# RE PURPOSED

THE
MEMOIRS OF
NEHEMIAH

## MIKE HURT

Published by LifeWay Press®
© 2008 Lifeway Press

No part of this work may be reproduced or transmitted in any form or
by any means, electronic or mechanical, including photocopying and
recording, or by any information storage or retrieval system, except as
may be expressly permitted in writing by the publisher. Requests for
permission should be addressed in writing to LifeWay Press®, One
LifeWay Plaza, Nashville, TN 37234-0175.

ISBN: 978-1415-8656-44
Item: 005153937

Dewey Decimal Classification Number: 307
Subject Heading: NEHEMIAH \ BIBLE. O.T. NEHEMIAH—STUDY \ COMMUNITY LIFE

Printed in the United States of America.

Leadership and Adult Publishing
LifeWay Church Resources
One LifeWay Plaza
Nashville, Tennessee 37234-0175

We believe the Bible has God for its author; salvation for its end; and truth,
without any mixture of error, for its matter and that all Scripture is totally true
and trustworthy. The 2000 statement of The Baptist Faith and Message is our
doctrinal guideline.

Unless otherwise indicated, all Scripture quotations are taken from the
Holman Christian Standard Bible®, copyright © 1999, 2000, 2002, 2003 by
Holman Bible Publishers. Used by permission. Holman Christian Standard
Bible®, Holman CSB®, and HCSB® are federally registered trademarks of
Holman Bible Publishers. Other versions include: Scripture quotations
marked The Message are taken from The Message. Copyright © by Eugene
H. Peterson, 1993, 1994, 1995, 1996, 2000, 2001, 2002. Used by permission of
NavPress Publishing Group.

Cover illustration and design by Brezinka Design Co. (brezinkadesign.com).
Inside photos by Rich Kalonick Photography (richkphoto.com).

# CONTENTS

## Meet the Author  Mike Hurt

My name is Mike, and I'm an author, dad, husband, and pastor. I live in Leesburg, Virginia, with my wife, Kristi, and our three kids. I am on staff at McLean Bible Church (*mcleanbible.org*) just outside of Washington, D.C. In my role as director of community campus development, I'm leading us to become one church with multiple locations. Day in and day out, I have the unique opportunity to lead our church to multiply and thrive throughout the D.C. area and to make sure as it does, people connect with each other in real, biblical community. That's what really excites me—seeing people follow the Lord together. That idea has been formative in this study as well as my first study for Threads, *Connect the Dots: Discovering God's Ongoing Will In Your Life*. Before moving to D.C., I was raised in Louisiana and then graduated with a Master of Divinity from Southwestern Baptist Theological Seminary.

Thanks for picking up a copy of *Repurposed*. As I wrote it, I discovered I have a new hero. His name is Nehemiah. Granted, I have been a fan of his for years from a distance. Since I am a pastor/leader in the church, I have always wanted to accomplish the types of things that Nehemiah did. But the closer I got to him, the less I wanted to do the things he did, and the more I wanted to be the man that he was. I want to be a man who courageously lives out my convictions no matter the setting. It's my prayer that as you study the life and memoirs of Nehemiah that God will bring about the same desire in you.

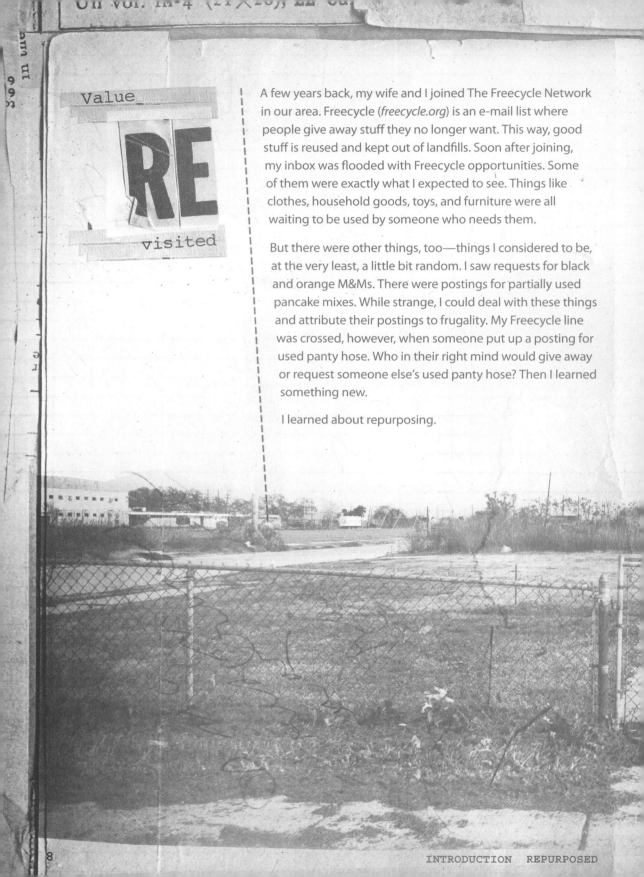

## Value revisited

A few years back, my wife and I joined The Freecycle Network in our area. Freecycle (*freecycle.org*) is an e-mail list where people give away stuff they no longer want. This way, good stuff is reused and kept out of landfills. Soon after joining, my inbox was flooded with Freecycle opportunities. Some of them were exactly what I expected to see. Things like clothes, household goods, toys, and furniture were all waiting to be used by someone who needs them.

But there were other things, too—things I considered to be, at the very least, a little bit random. I saw requests for black and orange M&Ms. There were postings for partially used pancake mixes. While strange, I could deal with these things and attribute their postings to frugality. My Freecycle line was crossed, however, when someone put up a posting for used panty hose. Who in their right mind would give away or request someone else's used panty hose? Then I learned something new.

I learned about repurposing.

Repurposing happens as you find an alternative use for something that already exists. Take panty hose for instance. There are a number of ways you can repurpose a pair. You can make a dress out of them. You can store onions or potatoes in them. You can cut them into strips and they become great stake ties for your garden. You can strain cheese through them. You can even create a great disguise by putting the panty hose over your head the next time you rob a bank. I think you get the point.

But it doesn't stop there. Repurposing has broader implications than just keeping good stuff out of our landfills. We see repurposing any time something we thought was only worth throwing away is suddenly reused. Repurposing also happens with communities and with people. It happens when we see our current lives in a new light.

In fact, it seems repurposing is about hope. This happens when we come to know Christ. He makes all things new. He repurposes us. It also happens as we follow Christ throughout our lives. He shows us how we can live out our convictions with clarity and compassion. He shows us ways to repurpose the world around us.

That is exactly what Nehemiah did. He repurposed his own life by following God's call to Jerusalem. He repurposed broken-down walls. He repurposed a community of faith that was far from God. He repurposed a city that was living disconnected from one another and suffering as a result. He repurposed political and social systems. In each of these repurposing efforts, he brought a new vision for what could be to what already existed.

Nehemiah brought hope.

Through the course of writing this study, I have grown in my respect for who Nehemiah was. Before looking closely at his life, I was more impressed by what he did than who he was. After all, he is arguably history's greatest builder. He accomplished an incredible feat of construction in a remarkably short time. But as I studied, I realized Nehemiah's character and commitment were far more impressive than his accomplishments. Don't get me wrong. He did some amazing things:

• He motivated the people to rebuild Jerusalem's walls in 52 days.
• He faced conflict and opposition with relational and personal integrity.
• He led God-centered reforms so that people would not be treated unjustly.
• He called everyone to return to God and to repent of their sin.

These accomplishments certainly put him in the company of world-class leaders, but these things are not what truly defined his life. Nehemiah's accomplishments were the result of his life being defined by God and grounded in His Word. His amazing deeds were the result of a man who didn't just see things as they were or even as they could be.

Nehemiah saw things as they *should* be and took action to make things right.

As you work through *Repurposed*, I hope you'll be challenged as I have. Specifically, I hope you will be forced to look in two directions. First, take a look at your own life as you study the life of Nehemiah. Look at the things that define you. Look intently at what drives you. See the places where you are living with integrity, and then notice where you are falling short. Second, focus outside of yourself. Where can you live your convictions with courage and compassion as you become a part of God's repurposing of the world around you?

Jesus is taking stuff some might consider only worth throwing away
and repurposing it for the glory of God. You can be a part of that.
So let's go dumpster-diving with Nehemiah. Let's not give up
on ourselves, God, or the church. Let's be a part of God's
recycling program.

I AM COMING HOME!
I WILL REBUILD!
I AM NEW ORLEANS!

So the rumors are true.

It's hard to believe it, but now there
is no doubt—the city of my grandfather,
and his father before him, and of
all God's people—lies in ruins. I'd
suspected as much, even heard pieces
of reports from time to time, but not
until today did it become real. Up
until today I've held onto the old
stories, stories about the glory and
the temple and the community. I've never
been there, of course, but everyone
tells stories. I guess I was holding
onto hope that the reports weren't as
bad as people were making them out
to be, like maybe if Jerusalem wasn't
destroyed that things could once again
be as they were before all the sin and
all the consequences. But I can no
longer ignore the truth.

Yet what can I do? I'm no general.
I'm no builder. I'm not really even
a leader. I serve wine. And unless
God intervenes, that's all I'll ever
do. Nevertheless, I cannot shake this
feeling—this prompting that is seeking
to convince me of my personal stake in
the future of a broken-down city and a
broken-down people. But what can I do?
For now, I can pray. And I can
wait...

                        - Nehemiah
                        445 B.C.

The name *Nehemiah* means, "the Lord has comforted." It's a pretty ironic name given Nehemiah's place in biblical history. He was displaced in a strange land, having landed there due to his people's disobedience. His name, however, is a reminder that even though the Israelites were deported to foreign nations due to their sin, God did not forget His people.

Not much else is known about Nehemiah's heritage other than his father's name. It is not mentioned anywhere else in the Old Testament. However, since almost 150 years had passed since Nebuchadnezzar and the Babylonians conquered Jerusalem, Hacaliah would have been born in exile, as would have his father before him.

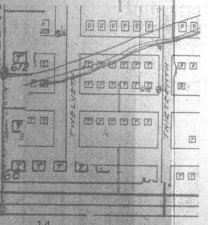

## ORDINARY RETHOUGHT

Church historians say, "Nehemiah was one of the great characters of the Old Testament; he should be ranked along with Moses and David as one of the creative personalities of Hebrew history."[1] What is the pedigree for a man known as one of the greatest leaders in the Bible? What was the background of one who could rebuild a city in 52 days? Nehemiah was a nobody before he was somebody. Look at how he was introduced in Nehemiah 1:1: "The words of Nehemiah son of Hacaliah."

His description tells us nothing special about him except that it distinguishes him from the other Nehemiahs of the Bible. Later, Nehemiah's title changes. He becomes "Nehemiah the governor, son of Hacaliah" (Nehemiah 10:1). But make no mistake about it, when God called him, he was simply Hacaliah's son Nehemiah. He was just another Jewish boy born during the period known as the exile, a time when the Israelites were deported initially to Babylon after centuries of sin.

There was no foreshadowing of future success as with other Old Testament heroes of the faith. No dreams like Joseph. No burning bush like Moses. No promises like Abraham. No anointing of future greatness like David. No elevation to royalty like Esther. No recruiting to the king's service like Daniel. Nehemiah was radically ordinary.

Nehemiah also lacked a supernatural mandate like we see in the New Testament. There was no angelic visit like Mary's or Damascus Road experience like Paul's. There were no mission-giving dreams like those Peter experienced. In many ways, Nehemiah was very much like you and me. He wrestled on a daily basis with what it meant to live out the call God had on his life. He worked through his call with fervent prayer and with risky faith just like you and I do. This gives me great hope, because if God can work through Nehemiah, then I know He can work through me as well.

**Do you tend to think of biblical characters as ordinary or extraordinary? Why?**

How do you think God wants you to view them?

Without exception in Scripture, you discover the hard, unvarnished truth about people. For example, David was a man of great courage and passion. He was also a man of great lust and anger. Samson knew what it felt like to have the strength of the Lord flowing through his body; he also knew what it was like to put his trust in the wrong people and how damaging pride can be. Moses was an incredible leader who knew unmatched intimacy with God; he was also presumptuous and hot-tempered. Peter had enough faith to walk on water but too little to confess Christ before a single child.

It's as if God is determined to point out that these "heroes" are just like us. They had their flaws because in the end, they were just regular people who put themselves in positions to be used by God. Their availability was more important than their ability, and the same is true for us.

## USABILITY

When he began writing his memoirs, Nehemiah was the cupbearer to the king of Persia. Being a cupbearer, or butler, for the king was a high-ranking office in the royal courts. It was Nehemiah's duty to serve wine and to ensure the king wasn't poisoned. When necessary, he would ensure the king's safety by drinking some of his wine before serving it. He was willing to lay his life down for the king, and that relationship put Nehemiah in a position God intended to use.

If you desire to be used greatly by God, do what Nehemiah did. Be faithful where God has put you and trust Him with the rest. Don't try to cheat, swindle, or steal your way to the top. God won't honor that. Instead, make it your number one goal to be available to God. Then look to see how and when God wants to use you. Don't miss this: You must be usable to be used by God. This is a strategy Nehemiah evidenced throughout his memoirs—we see acknowledgment of God's guidance (2:8,18); concern for divine blessing (5:19; 6:14; 13:14,22,29,31); and frequent prayers (1:5-11; 2:4; 4:4-5:9; 6:9).[2]

Persian kings had to deal with the same problem of any monarch—the threat of assassination. The cupbearer not only brought the wine to the king but often tasted it to test for poison. This was a position of the highest trust, and often there was a strong bond between the two.

Availability is more important to God than ability. Take the 12 ordinary, fishermen turned disciples, for example. Check out John MacArthur's *Twelve Ordinary Men* for more about how God used nobodies to turn the world upside down.

When I think of what God looks for in a leader, I think Nehemiah epitomizes what Jesus says in Luke 16:10-12. I love the way The Message translation puts it:

**If you're honest in small things,**
  **you'll be honest in big things;**
**If you're a crook in small things,**
  **you'll be a crook in big things.**
**If you're not honest in small jobs,**
  **who will put you in charge of the store?**

The bottom line from this passage, and exhibited in Nehemiah's life, is that God honors faithfulness. He honors us with more responsibility and influence when we honor Him with the smallest pieces of our lives.

**What are the small things in your life?**

**How are you expressing faithfulness in the small things?**

Through the Book of Nehemiah, "We can trace the voluntary assumption of responsibility and initiative in the midst of a social crisis by an individual whom God called and equipped for leadership, and whom men thereupon recognized and followed."[3]

Nehemiah was set apart from the crowd by both his character and work ethic. Nehemiah would never have had the opportunity to rise from insignificance to a cupbearer of the king had he been a lazy, good-for-nothing person. To get this job, he had to be just the opposite. The faithfulness he demonstrated as a cupbearer would become the hallmark quality of each of his future leadership positions. His ability to remain faithful even in the face of difficulties and opposition ensured that he remained usable by God.

According to Jim Collins' best seller, *Good to Great*, the most effective leaders in our world exhibit "a paradoxical blend of personal humility and professional will."[4] Collins describes great leaders as "cut from the same cloth. It didn't matter whether the company was consumer or industrial, in a crisis or a steady state, offered services or products. Nor did it matter when the transition took place or the size of the company."[5]

One of the ways this leadership is demonstrated is through their "unwavering resolve" to do whatever must be done to produce the best long-term results, no matter how difficult the process. A great leader "acts with quiet, calm determination" and "relies principally on inspired standards, not inspiring charisma, to motivate."[6] I love it when the world catches up with the Bible and biblical leadership qualities are endorsed even by people who don't know Christ. It reinforces the fact that God's Word addresses every area of our lives, even our leadership and influence. If you are looking to move your leadership from good to great, study Nehemiah and pattern your life after him. Put yourself in a position to be usable by God, and then look for every opportunity for Him to use you.

**What do you think a totally usable person looks like?**

**Are there areas of your life that you need to change to make you usable?**

*Good to Great* by Jim Collins has emerged as a definitive work examining how organizations move from standard to excellent. It provides a helpful framework for both the secular and sacred.

## NEHEMIAH'S CONTEXT

We can't truly understand a man or a woman without understanding the world in which he or she lived. Nehemiah lived in very turbulent times to say the least. His family was a part of the 4,600 Jewish people exiled to Babylon as a part of Nebuchadnezzar's march against Jerusalem in 586 B.C. (Jeremiah 52:28ff). It was in this assault on Jerusalem that the city walls were demolished, the huge wooden city gates were burned down, and the temple was destroyed. All but the poorest of the poor were relocated from Jerusalem.

They remained in captivity until 538 B.C., when the Persians overtook Babylon, and Cyrus the Great released some 42,000 of the Jews and allowed them to return to Jerusalem (Ezra 2:64). Those who returned to Jerusalem found little success upon their arrival. Attempts to reconstruct the temple were short-lived as a result of opposition.

It wasn't until Haggai and Zechariah appeared a few years later and encouraged people to get to work again that Jerusalem began to be restored. Sixty more years passed, and more Israelites returned to Jerusalem under Ezra's leadership to complete the rebuilding of the temple in 515 B.C.[7] Even with the temple restored, there was still much work to be done in Jerusalem. The walls lay in shambles. When Nehemiah returned to Jerusalem in 445 B.C, rebuilding the walls was an issue of national security and pride.[8]

**How do you think the people felt when they looked at their broken walls?**

**Can you relate to that feeling? How?**

The *exile* of the Israelites occurred in 586 B.C. Biblically, the terms *exile* and *captivity* are used to mean the same thing. The terms refer to the deportation of peoples in the ancient world for political reasons. By removing people from their homeland, a nation's power was destroyed, and the conquering nation could resettle the land with its allies. Spiritually, the exile came about as a result of centuries of disobedience and idolatry.

The city walls weren't the only problem. They were in many ways symbolic of the spiritual and physical condition of the people of God. During the exile, some left their faith as they were taken to Babylon. They picked up the beliefs of the pagan cultures around them. They even married outside of the Jewish people.

Not only were people struggling spiritually, they were also struggling physically. One of the main purposes of the walls was protection against enemies. With no walls, there was no certainty of safety. With no protection, there was limited commerce, meaning limited food and supplies. Over time, this resulted in severe famine. This was the Jerusalem that Nehemiah was called to rebuild—a city and a community of people in shambles.

At first glance, it may be difficult for us to relate to the world in which Nehemiah lived, but a deeper look shows a world we cannot only relate to, but live in every day. Because of the exile, many people merged their God-centered beliefs with the pagan beliefs of neighboring countries, resulting in a less than pure biblical faith. God's people abandoned the call of the Lord to live purely, to be a part of society responsible for introducing the rest of the world to God by their customs, actions, and lifestyles. Likewise, you and I live in a world of moral relativism that rejects all forms of absolute truth, especially in regard to the person of Jesus Christ.

Because of the exile, men, women, and children lived desolate, poverty-stricken lives. In the fall of 2005, we witnessed the same thing as the poorest of the poor paid the highest price when Hurricane Katrina came ashore. That's just one example of the significant gap between the rich and the poor that still exists today and only worsens through natural disasters, war, and political unrest. Because of the exile, Jerusalem was in need of both physical and spiritual renewal. One can hardly deny that our world needs the same. This is the world you and I are living in. Our world. Nehemiah's world.

**When you think about the similarities between our world and Nehemiah's world, what stands out to you?**

Half the world—nearly three billion people—live on less than two dollars a day. The GDP (Gross Domestic Product) of the poorest 48 nations (i.e. a quarter of the world's countries) is less than the wealth of the world's three richest people combined..

Nearly a billion people entered the 21st century unable to read a book or sign their names. Less than one percent of what the world was spending every year at that time on weapons was needed to put every child into school by the year 2000, and yet it didn't happen. For more statistics on issues around the world today check out *globalissues.org*.

## NEHEMIAH'S MESSAGE

Nehemiah's message is one of commitment, hope, and renewal. He wasn't a politician looking for governmental change. Nor was he a preacher looking for religious revival. He wasn't a military leader looking for victory. He was all three. But in each of these roles, there was a common thread we need to recognize. He did what he did in order to build up the people of God. He wasn't building a wall, a church, or an army. Nehemiah was building biblical community.

In a world where the people of God were dispersed and often alone, Nehemiah brought them together. In a world where the people of God had turned away from Him, Nehemiah called them back to faith. In a world where the name of God was being mocked, he returned honor to the Lord's name. Nehemiah understood that "the work of building community is the noblest work a person can do."[9]

His central message was one of dependence. He called the people to depend on the hand of God as they rebuilt the walls. Nehemiah called the people to depend on God and trust His Word as he led them through political and social reform. He called the people to depend on God as he led them to be spiritually right through straight-forward teaching of the law, confession, and celebration.

We should learn not only from Nehemiah's message, but also from how he lived and delivered that message. Throughout our study, you will see a level of integrity in Nehemiah's life that is seldom matched, even in biblical literature. His integrity and personal commitment to God were the secrets to the success of his ministry in Jerusalem.

We will also see a highly relational leader as we study Nehemiah. This relational leadership style was substantially different than any of the leaders before him. Through this relational foundation, Nehemiah understood the needs of the people and was able to teach them how to meet the needs of one another. Relational leaders are often people-pleasers, but not Nehemiah. He was a leader who was willing to make risky calls to commitment and face opposition head on.

I believe Nehemiah demonstrated each of these qualities because he identified personally with the mission God called him to. This is exemplified in the fact that he was a "we" and an "us" leader rather than a "you" and "them" leader. We all have been around "you" and "them" leaders. They are the type of leaders who point out everyone else's problems. They're quick

Henri Nouwen's book *In the Name of Jesus* provides a radical framework for leadership, a design in which the leader needs his or her people as much as the people need their leader. Pick up a copy of this short book to read more.

to tell you what you should be doing while not talking about their personal contribution. They distance themselves from people and from the mission with their "you/them" thinking. If a pastor is this type of a leader, people may often leave church feeling like he has it all together while their lives are a wreck. He's a super-Christian and you feel as though you rank somewhere just below pond scum. This type of leadership won't last and won't produce the type of fruit that we see in Nehemiah's service to the Lord.

> **Why do you think it's so crucial for leaders to relate to their people?**

> **Is there any danger in doing so?**

> **How can a leader guard against those dangers?**

*"So if I, your Lord and Teacher, have washed your feet, you also ought to wash one another's feet. For I have given you an example that you also should do just as I have done for you" (John 13:14-15).*

We must strive to replace "you/them" thinking with "us/we" thinking. Nehemiah did this by identifying with the sin of Israel:

> **" . . . let Your eyes be open and Your ears be attentive to hear Your servant's prayer that I now pray to You day and night for Your servants, the Israelites. I confess the sins we have committed against You. Both I and my father's house have sinned" (Nehemiah 1:6).**

Even in his personal time in prayer, Nehemiah applied the "us/we" thinking. He could have blamed the people for their condition as he prayed, but he didn't. He knit his heart with theirs through his prayer of confession. When he came against his chief opposers, Sanballat the Horonite, Tobiah the Ammonite official, and Geshem the Arab, he once again showed that his leadership was more about "we" than "me." See how he responded to their mocking:

> **"I gave them this reply, 'The God of heaven is the One who will grant us success. We, His servants, will start building . . ."** (Nehemiah 2:20).

God gave Nehemiah a vision for the future, but God gave everyone the success because they were led by an "us/we" leader.

For articles, tips, and perspective from fellow community builders visit the daily blog at *threadsmedia.com*.

### NEHEMIAH'S ACCOMPLISHMENTS

Four times in his memoirs Nehemiah asked God to remember his actions. As we begin our study of Nehemiah, it is important for us to understand what Nehemiah wanted God to remember. In doing so, we will learn about him from the inside-out. Take a moment and read the following passages:

- Nehemiah 5:14-19
- Nehemiah 13:6-14
- Nehemiah 13:15-22
- Nehemiah 13:23-31

Each of these were times of intense struggle and faith-filled action on Nehemiah's part. These were not self-centered requests by Nehemiah. He wasn't trying to earn brownie points with God. These "remember me" requests were more of a last ditch act of faith. These requests are representative of the difficulty he was facing and are a clear indication of his trust in God. These requests are also mile markers in Nehemiah's life and points at which I am certain he looked back and gave thanks to God.

Through these requests we also begin to see the major themes of the life and ministry of Nehemiah emerge. We see a man who exemplifies what it means to be a servant leader. We see a man who is committed to godliness and the restoration of Israel. We see a man who not only stands for truth personally but also leads others to apply Scripture to their lives. We see a man who models what many of us would be proud to become someday.

**Does it bother you that Nehemiah asked God to remember his actions? Why or why not?**

**Would it bother you to do the same? Why or why not?**

As you look at the life of Nehemiah, don't fall prey to the idea that all of these accomplishments make him a larger than life person. Nehemiah was human, just like us. As you read his memoirs, I hope that you will see just how normal he was. Too many times, we inflate our perspective of biblical heroes. Think back to the story of David and Goliath.

Who was the giant—David or Goliath? Of course, Goliath was the giant. He stood more than 9-feet tall. He was the man whose mere threats left Saul and his army dismayed and terrified. David was the shepherd boy who couldn't even fill Saul's armor. David was the one who had nothing but five smooth stones, a sling, and great faith. So what's the point in all of this? One of the takeaways from the lives of David and Nehemiah is that God does the extraordinary with the ordinary. God finds His heroes in very unlikely places and uses them in very unlikely ways.

To refresh your memory, read the full account of David versus Goliath in 1 Samuel 17.

Does this encourage you as much as it does me? I am convinced we can do the same things that Nehemiah did to be used by God. God may choose to use us in different ways, but the things Nehemiah did to be usable are universal. This is one of the reasons we should study the life and words of Nehemiah—to know how to best position ourselves to be used by God. When we study the Book of Nehemiah, we learn not only about Nehemiah, but we also learn about the God he followed.

God's covenant with Israel was established on Mount Sinai (Exodus 19). Covenants were binding agreements in legal, marriage, and religious contexts. This covenant expressed God's love for His people and His desire to dwell with them, as does the new covenant which was ratified with Christ's blood.

We see that God is One who keeps His promises. In Leviticus 26 and in Deuteronomy 27-30, we learn God made a covenant with His people, promising blessings if they obeyed but discipline if they refused to listen to Him. The city of Jerusalem was in ruins because of the sins of the people. As you think about a God who keeps His word, don't just ask why God would punish people to the extent that He did. Instead, focus on His desire to bless His people and stand confident that if He keeps His promise to punish, He will also keep His promise to bless.

We also see that God is bigger than any opposition we may face. When the city walls were rebuilt to half their height, the opposition turned up the heat, but Nehemiah's trust in the Lord didn't wane:

> **"When Sanballat, Tobiah, and the Arabs, Ammonites, and Ashdodites heard that the repair to the walls of Jerusalem was progressing and that the gaps were being closed, they became furious. They all plotted together to come and fight against Jerusalem and throw it into confusion. So we prayed to our God and stationed a guard because of them day and night"** (Nehemiah 4:7-9).

Their first step in facing the opposition was to pray. Yes, they took an additional step of posting guards, but don't miss what they did first—they trusted God, their true protector. Nehemiah knew that God was bigger than any of his opposition. If he was trusting God, he didn't have to fear any man.

We also see a God who comes through in very tangible ways. Nehemiah trusted the hand of God to protect and strengthen the people as they rebuilt the walls. The co-laborers were in a position that if God didn't come through, they were destined to fail. They were doomed without God. But with Him, they were positioned to do the miraculous. Together, they rebuilt the city's walls in 52 days. God came through with His protection and strength.

It is my prayer that through our study you will see the opportunities God has put before you. I hope that you first see the opportunities through the character of God. This is the starting point, because it is unchanging and gives us our marching orders. I also hope that you will see how you can grasp every opportunity God puts before you—just as Nehemiah did. This framework for living will repurpose your life.

I also hope that you will examine both your ability to lead and your ability to follow. You can't have one without the other. As we'll look at later, every leader is following someone, especially if we claim to be Christ-following leaders. Warren Wiersbe poses some specific questions from the life of Nehemiah that we should all reflect on throughout this study:

## QUESTIONS AS WE LEAD:

Like Nehemiah, do you have a burden in your heart for the work God has called you to do? Why or why not?

Are you willing to sacrifice to see His will accomplished? How important is God's will to you?

Preacher and commentator Warren Weirsbe titled his work on Nehemiah *Be Determined*. It captures the need for perseverance in the face of opposition and God's desire to do the seemingly miraculous through His people.

Are you patient in gathering facts and planning our work, or do you charge in too quickly? Why is patience important?

Do you enlist the help of others or try to do everything yourself? Why do you tend to lean one way or the other?

Do you motivate people on the basis of the spiritual—what God is doing—or simply on the basis of the personal? Why?

Are they following You or the Lord as He leads you?

## QUESTIONS AS WE FOLLOW:

Do you listen to what your leaders say and share their burdens, or do often resent their authority? Why?

Do you cling to the past or desire to see God do something new? Why?

Do you put your hands and your neck to the work, or are you prone to hold back? Why?

Are you cooperating in any way with the enemy and fighting against God's working among us? In what ways do you support each?

Listen to "We Build" by Nichole Nordeman from the *Repurposed* playlist. Your group leader can send you the playlist via e-mail, or you can download it at *threadsmedia.com/media.*

## THE WALLS ARE GOING UP

We should not only look at the personal implications from Nehemiah. We should also look for lessons to be applied to the biblical community we are a part of. Remember, Nehemiah wasn't just building a wall or a city. He was building a community.

The church of today needs Nehemiah. I don't mean this in a pessimistic way. Some see the church today and see little to celebrate but much to criticize. Not me. Sure, the church needs to be repurposed in some places. Specifically from Nehemiah, we know that every church should be led by leaders who are fully surrendered to God's call on their lives.

We see that churches should practice biblical compassion by both noticing and meeting the needs of people around them. We also know that our commitment to community should be about what we give and what we get as a result of our connection. And we see that the church should call men and women to decompartmentalize their lives so they can be usable by God. As we face these challenges and seek reform in our communities, we need to do so with hopeful optimism, because it is God who we are trusting to accomplish all of this. The walls are going up again.

# session one  - Building Blocks
-----------------------------------------------------------------

Throughout your study of *Repurposed*, you will
find a section at the close of every chapter
containing building blocks designed to enrich
your study. Through these practices, you will
be able to dwell more deeply on Nehemiah's
message and move further in God's design for a
repurposed life.

The Building Blocks contain key readings from
Nehemiah, broken down so you can use them
as devotional reading between your sessions;
a Scripture to memorize that captures a key
idea from the previous session; and a specific
challenge for how you can actively practice the
principles you are learning.

Pick up a brick.

## Read

* Day 1     Nehemiah 1:1-11
* Day 2     Nehemiah 2:1-10
* Day 3     Nehemiah 2:11-20
* Day 4     Nehemiah 3:1-12
* Day 5     Nehemiah 3:13-19

## Memorize

"Whoever is faithful in very little is also faithful in much, and whoever is unrighteous in very little is also unrighteous in much. So if you have not been faithful with the unrighteous money, who will trust you with what is genuine?" (Luke 16:10-11).

## Challenge

Nehemiah often asked God to remember his actions, the ways Nehemiah had been faithful to God's direction and calling in the past— even in the little things. Spend some time evaluating your own faithfulness. Detail your week on paper. Include things you might consider to be "small" such as eating, watching movies, surfing the net. Then consider how comfortable you are in asking God to remember your actions in those little things. Record your thoughts.

LINEA MEXICAN

SESSION ONE REPURPOSED

upper 9th ward, New Orleans, LA

# session 2 - Leadership Reimagined

I arrived today and saw the situation for myself. Hanani was right; it's bad. The city is in horrible shape. It's as if people have given up and are just waiting around for the next day to come. That's the worst part—not the rubble and the falling down walls, but the state of the people. I look out at them and see people so desperately looking for someone to lead them that they don't even realize they are looking. They are like sheep without a shepherd.

And I am one of them. I'm not high and mighty, the grand savior from Persia sent to rescue their city and their lives. I'm just as insecure, just as needy, just as broken as the people sleeping in the streets. Is there a way for us to come together, not under my leadership, but under God's? Is there a way for them to follow me as they walk with me? Is there a way for me to be both one of their own and their leader? I think there is. I pray there is—for all our sakes. More later . . .

## LEADERSHIP REIMAGINED

I've always struggled with what it means to be a spiritual leader. I heard I was supposed to be a spiritual leader when I was dating my wife. Did that mean any more than I should keep my hands to myself? I think so, but beyond that I wasn't always sure how to flesh it out. As a pastor, I'm supposed to be a spiritual leader. Does that mean that I am a professional Christian? I sure hope not. As a dad, I'm supposed to be a spiritual leader. Does that mean I pray before dinner and make my kids go to church? There has to be more to spiritual leadership than this stuff.

**What's the difference in *leadership* and *spiritual leadership*?**

**How do you define *spiritual leadership*?**

John Piper defines *spiritual leadership* as "knowing where God wants people to be and taking the initiative to use God's methods to get them there in reliance on God's power." You can read the full transcript of his article at *desiringgod.org* by searching for "spiritual leadership."

If you have similar questions or frustrations, take heart because Nehemiah teaches all of us what it looks like to be a spiritual leader. What we see in his life is a rare level of spiritual commitment and consistency. We see a man who loved God deeply and allowed that love to infect every area of his life. We see a man who was brave enough to answer God's call to do something impossible. We see a spiritual leader.

We can look at Nehemiah's leadership life from two perspectives. We can find broad principles every leader of every age can learn from, but we can also glean some leadership steps specifically for young adult leaders.

In a broad sense, I see three lessons all Christ-followers can apply to their lives if they want to be spiritual leaders:
1. Don't speak *for* God until you speak *with* God.
2. Don't speak *for* God until you hear *from* God.
3. Take responsibility for the spiritual growth of others.

If our leaders get this right they will have no shortage of followers, because godly people follow godly leaders who have godly intentions.

## THE CART BEFORE THE HORSE

We see the first principle come out following a conversation between Nehemiah and his brother Hanani in Nehemiah 1. Hanani had just come to Persia from Judah. When Nehemiah saw his brother, he did what you or I would do—he asked about home. He asked his brother about the Jewish remnant that survived the exile, and he asked about Jerusalem, the once glorious center of the people of God. These questions demonstrate Nehemiah's focus—he was concerned about God's people and about God's place. Unfortunately, he received bad news on both fronts. As for God's people, they were in a dire state. Hanani told him that they were "in great trouble and disgrace" (Nehemiah 1:3). The news on God's place, Jerusalem, was not any better. The walls were broken down and the gates were burned.

So what? So the gates were burned and the walls were busted up. Jerusalem had been sacked after all. Why should these things matter so much to Nehemiah? There must have been a lot of reasons. The walls were the source of protection for the city, so without them, it was virtually impossible for those living inside to function with much security and safety. The gates were essential for commerce, rendering the trade of goods and services limited at best. But there's something more, too. Jerusalem had been a beacon of hope for the Jewish people—Nehemiah's people. It was God's city. It was the city of the sacrifices, the priesthood, the very center of Jewish cultural and religious life. And now it sat in ruins—much like how many people saw their relationship with God.

The news hit Nehemiah like a Mac truck. He was about to find what Bill Hybels calls his "holy discontent." This was his Popeye moment—the moment where he has all he can stands and he can't stands no more.[10] For nearly a century his people must have been saying, "Somebody ought to do something about those walls." Others must have replied, "We've tried and nothing can be done." It was different with Nehemiah, though. Because of his character, Nehemiah felt responsible to take some action. He was reduced to tears. These tears turned to God-centered mourning and fasting. This period of mourning and fasting was not a grab for attention or an escape from the reality of the situation. It was an opportunity for him to talk to God before he talked to anyone else or took any action.

His mourning and fasting led him to a focused time of prayer and trusting in God. We see this prayer in Nehemiah 1:5-7:

Under the leadership of Zerubbabel, about 70 years before Nehemiah returned to Jerusalem, some progress in rebuilding the city had been made. But slowly the temple and sacrifices were neglected, and the Jews had once again adopted the religious practices of the surrounding nations—the very sin that led to the exile in the first place.

Bill Hybels, the founding pastor of Willow Creek Community Church, is a prolific author and speaker. His latest book, *Just Walk Across the Room*, is a call for everyday people to take practical, easy, and relational steps to extend the kingdom of God.

**"LORD God of heaven, the great and awe-inspiring God who keeps His gracious covenant with those who love Him and keep His commands, let Your eyes be open and Your ears be attentive to hear Your servant's prayer that I now pray to You day and night for Your servants, the Israelites. I confess the sins we have committed against You. Both I and my father's house have sinned. We have acted corruptly toward You and have not kept the commands, statutes, and ordinances You gave Your servant Moses."**

What an amazing pattern for prayer we can learn from Nehemiah's words.

Nehemiah began by focusing on the awesome nature of God. He recognized that He is a loving God who keeps His commitments to those who love and obey Him. I don't know about you, but when I face challenges a fraction of the size of what Nehemiah was facing, I struggle to trust God like he did. It's not necessarily an overt lack of trust; it's much more subtle. And my trust—or distrust—of God is expressed through how I pray.

I show my lack of trust by starting with me and my needs instead of starting with God and His character. I'm so preoccupied with my needs and so worried about what's happening that I rush to get there in my prayers. I rush to get there, that is, when I actually choose to pray first. Notice that Nehemiah's first response was prayer.

My temptation when I encounter a problem is to immediately spring into physical action. Not Nehemiah—he prayed, and he didn't just pray for a moment. He committed himself to a season of prayer, petitioning the Lord "for a number of days" (Nehemiah 1:4). The amount of days and nights doesn't matter; what does matter is that he committed himself to an extended time of focused prayer. I struggle with this because I think I should be *doing* something rather than "just praying." Did you catch the problem with my last sentence? The problem is that it is impossible to "just pray." The prayer life of a leader matters more than we will ever know.

**Do you consider prayer to be preparation for the work or the work itself? Why?**

Resources on prayer abound in the Christian world. Richard Foster offers an extensive but very readable resource, simply titled *Prayer*, that will stretch your understanding of what it means to encounter God.

After Nehemiah focused on the nature of God, he asked God to hear him and to see his commitment. He prayed:

> **"Let Your eyes be open and Your ears be attentive to hear Your servant's prayer that I now pray to You day and night for Your servants, the Israelites. I confess the sins we have committed against You. Both I and my father's house have sinned"** (Nehemiah 1:6).

That's a pretty bold move. What was the source of this boldness? I think Nehemiah understood that God wants to meet the needs of His children. Jesus taught us the same thing:

> **"Keep asking, and it will be given to you. Keep searching, and you will find. Keep knocking, and the door will be opened to you. For everyone who asks receives, and the one who searches finds, and to the one who knocks, the door will be opened. What man among you, if his son asks him for bread, will give him a stone? Or if he asks for a fish, will give him a snake? If you then, who are evil, know how to give good gifts to your children, how much more will your Father in heaven give good things to those who ask Him! Therefore, whatever you want others to do for you, do also the same for them—this is the Law and the Prophets"** (Matthew 7:7-12).

Matthew 7 is the conclusion of the Sermon on the Mount, Jesus' most extensive sermon detailing what a Christ-follower looks like in practical life.

Trusting the heart of God when we pray leads us to bold prayer even when the odds are stacked against us. But I think Nehemiah's prayer was also bold because he knew his motives were pure. When your motives are clean, you can pray for anything unapologetically. My guess is there have been times when you have prayed for something hesitantly—I have too. Even as I prayed, I wondered to myself, *Should I be praying this?*

This is one of the ways the Spirit of God teaches us what *not* to pray. Nehemiah's motives were pure. I know his motives were pure because he was praying for others instead of praying for himself. It's next to impossible to be self-centered when you are praying for someone else, especially if when God blesses them, you get nothing in return.

It's never easy to wait. To find principles of how to wait well, consider *In Transit: What Do You Do With Your Wait?* for your next small group study. Find more information at *threadsmedia.com*.

## WAIT

Nehemiah next turned his prayer to the spiritual condition of the Israelites. His confession shows that he knew the root of Israel's problems. When others saw broken-down walls and charred gates, he saw the city's spiritual condition. He was a man of incredible depth:

> **"I confess the sins we have committed against You. Both I and my father's house have sinned. We have acted corruptly toward You and have not kept the commands, statutes, and ordinances You gave Your servant Moses" (Nehemiah 1:6-7).**

The true problem wasn't a broken-down city filled with broken-down people. The true problem was a broken-down relationship with God. Nehemiah confessed the truth and trusted God's mercy for the rest.

> **How often do you pray for the spiritual needs of the people around you—your friends, neighbors, co-workers, and family?**

> **What keeps you from doing so more often?**

Born in 1828, Andrew Murray spent 60 years of ministry in the Dutch Reformed Church of South Africa. He also wrote more than 200 books and tracts on Christian spirituality and ministry, did extensive social work, and founded several educational institutions.

Before we move on, I want to make sure you catch this—Nehemiah showed us that a leader must bend a knee and wait on the Lord. Waiting on the Lord is a powerful stance for a leader. Andrew Murray describes why:

"In waiting on God, the first thought is of the God on whom we wait. We enter His presence and feel we need to be quiet so that He, as God, can overshadow us with Himself. God longs to reveal Himself and fill us with Himself. Waiting on God gives Him time in His own way and divine power to come to us."[11]

> **Why do you think it's so difficult to wait on God's timing?**

Is there a situation right now where you need to wait on the Lord?

Not only did Nehemiah find power in waiting on God, he also found wisdom as he turned to God. As Andrew Murray says, "Not till we have become humble and teachable, standing in awe of God's holiness and sovereignty, acknowledging our own littleness, distrusting our own thoughts and willing to have our minds turned upside down, can divine wisdom become ours."[12]

## VISION QUEST

After the work of prayer began the work of vision. Nehemiah knew he had a mandate from God to rebuild the walls. He didn't speak for God until he heard from God. He knew that God was on his side, but he didn't come in with all of the answers. Take a look at what he did:

> **"After I arrived in Jerusalem and had been there three days, I got up at night and took a few men with me. I didn't tell anyone what my God had laid on my heart to do for Jerusalem" (Nehemiah 2:11-12).**

He came in and inspected what reality was. Given Nehemiah's commitment to prayer, my guess is that he talked with God as he surveyed the situation. He wanted to see with his eyes and hear with his ears exactly what God was calling him to do. Once he knew what reality was, he cast vision for what the future could look like:

> **"So I said to them, 'You see the trouble we are in. Jerusalem lies in ruins and its gates have been burned down. Come let's rebuild Jerusalem's wall, so that we will no longer be a disgrace.' I told them how the gracious hand of God had been on me, and what the king had said to me" (Nehemiah 2:17-18).**

Because he heard from God, Nehemiah could speak for God. Because he heard from God, his vision was clear, compelling, and included everyone. His vision was right on, and so was his method for reaching his vision. He wasn't trusting his own leadership or the skills of the people. He was trusting God alone.

Andy Stanley, founding pastor of North Point Community Church, wrote *Visioneering* as an examination of the characteristics of a visionary leader found in Nehemiah.

Listen to "Work to Be Done" by Steven Delopoulos from the *Repurposed* playlist. Your group leader can send your the playlist via e-mail, or you can download it at *threadsmedia.com/media.*

How good are you at waiting on the Lord both for what you should do and for what you should say?

What does the pace of your life reveal about your relationship with the Lord?

I believe this is one of the tests for spiritual leadership. Can vision be cast and caught in such a way that all of God's people are involved and God gets all of the credit? This means the leader's motives and mission have to be pure. It also means that when the vision is being lived out, an ultimate dependence on God must be shown. The leader also gives God credit through the whole process.

This is essential because any vision of God is going to come with some opposition. It's not always as easy as it seems to live the vision God has given to you. Even Nehemiah experienced opposition to his God-sized, God-centered vision:

To read more about the opposition Nehemiah faced during his building, check out Nehemiah 4:1-5 and 6:1-9.

> **"When Sanballat the Horonite, Tobiah the Ammonite official, and Geshem the Arab heard about this, they mocked and despised us, and said, 'What is this you're doing? Are you rebelling against the king?' I gave them this reply, 'The God of heaven is the One who will grant us success. We, His servants, will start building, but you have no share, right, or historic claim in Jerusalem'" (Nehemiah 2:19-20).**

He dealt with his opposition straight up and showed once again who he was trusting for future success—the God of heaven. Spiritual leaders don't shrink back from opposition. They don't try to spin the situation to satisfy others. If you've heard from God, you can speak boldly for God and face any opposition.

## MY BROTHER'S KEEPER

With this type of foundation, a leader is ready to set an example worth following. This is the truest act of spiritual leadership because spiritual leaders take responsibility for other's growth. Nehemiah wasn't just focused on reconstructing the city. He also wanted Israel to have a restored relationship with God. Remember, to him the city's condition was a representation of the Jews' relationship with God.

As such, he took responsibility for the spiritual growth of the people. We see this in Nehemiah 13. After the Israelites returned from the exile and Nehemiah restored security and order to Jerusalem, he returned to the service of King Artaxerxes of Babylon. Notice the humility and faithfulness that this return to Babylon presented. He had spent 20 years rebuilding and repopulating the city. He could have remained in Jerusalem and enjoyed the fruit of his labor, but he couldn't do that and keep his word to the king. Remember, he had permission from the king to rebuild the city—not to stay there forever.

As a man of integrity, he knew he should return to the king's service. After serving for the king for a time, Nehemiah asked to return to Jerusalem. I can only imagine how his thoughts drifted toward Jerusalem while he was in Babylon. Upon his return to Jerusalem, he found that the house of God was not in order as he had left it.

Much like Jesus cleared the temple in Mark 11, Nehemiah cleaned house. He cleared out Tobiah and all of his gear, purified the room, and replaced the articles of worship. Next he turned his attention to the Levites and singers who had returned to their fields. They left their post as worship leaders because their portions of grain, new wine, and oil had not been given. In response, Nehemiah called everyone together and he rebuked the leaders. With a simple yet pointed question, "Why has the house of God been neglected?" (Nehemiah 13:11), Nehemiah set the stewardship bar high, and everyone gave as commanded.

Following this bold move, Nehemiah voiced a prayer that anyone committed to the church can relate to. I can imagine him tired and somewhat discouraged as he turned his eyes to heaven and said:

> **"Remember me for this, my God, and don't erase the good deeds I have done for the house of my God and for its services"** (Nehemiah 13:14).

The temple was an integral part of the life of Israel. Though one building obviously cannot contain the presence of God, the temple was a symbol of God's desire to dwell among and with His people. The destruction of the temple at the onset of the exile was a devastating moment for the people of God.

The word *tithe* means "tenth," and is the custom of returning a tenth portion of income to the Lord. The first recorded biblical tithe comes from Genesis 14:18-20, when Abraham gave a tenth of the spoils of war to the priest-king Melchizedek. Tithing remains a practice in Christianity as a sign of devotion to God and as a means to recognize God's ownership of everything.

This prayer was not only for what he had just done by restoring the tithe. It was also for what was about to come next. His reform work was not done.

Nehemiah's next act showed he believed every word and command of God; unfortunately, however, not everyone in Jerusalem believed and lived as he did. There were some who were neglecting or fully ignoring the Sabbath. Instead of taking a day to rest and worship, as commanded, they continued business as usual:

> **"At that time I saw people in Judah treading wine presses on the Sabbath. They were also bringing in stores of grain and loading them on donkeys, along with wine, grapes, and figs. All kinds of goods were being brought to Jerusalem on the Sabbath day. So I warned them against selling food on that day" (Nehemiah 13:15).**

In response, Nehemiah ordered that the gates of the city be shut and that no one could bring a load into Jerusalem on the Sabbath. If people weren't willing to live in obedience, he would protect them from themselves and close the city to trade traffic. Some tried to test his decree and camped outside of Jerusalem. Nehemiah personally addressed the campers by telling them he would "use force against" them if they ever did it again (Nehemiah 13:21). Apparently, this WWE style warning was more than enough because the meddling merchants never set up another tent.

**Do you think Nehemiah was overreacting? Why or why not?**

For statistics about biblical literacy and the spiritual climate of the 21st century, visit *lifewayresearch.com*.

If the producers of a recent remake of the classic film, *The Ten Commandments*, are right, we need to take the very same stand for each other's spiritual growth. Producers of the movie found Americans know more about the Big Mac than they do God's commandments. A whopping 80 percent of the respondents knew that the Big Mac had "two all-beef patties," yet only 60 percent knew that "thou shalt not kill" was on God's top 10 list. Only 29 percent knew about God's commandment forbidding false idols, and 34 percent knew the one about remembering the Sabbath.[13]

So how can you and I take responsibility for the growth of others? It starts with a mind-set. I must decide I'm going to live my life—every part—in such a way that if others follow me, they will become more like Christ. Paul made a bold statement in 1 Corinthians 11:1: "Be imitators of me, as I also am of Christ." This is the type of leadership we can provide today. We can be leaders who are distinctly Christian. We can lead in and outside of the church in such a way that our relationships with Christ affect our leadership lives.

Paul lived this, and he taught us how to do the same. He made it clear that his leadership authority came because he was following Christ. His leadership strategies were God-centered because he was following Christ. His methods for living out his leadership were consistent with Jesus' ministry because he was following Christ. Not only did Paul follow Christ's example, but he called us to do the same. He said to follow him as he followed Christ. That's what spiritual leaders do—they live a life worth following and then invite others to follow suit.

**How would you feel if someone tried to imitate your life? Why?**

## FOLLOW THE FOLLOWER

Right now, you may be thinking, *I'm not Paul, and I'm not sure that I am the one to follow.* It worked for Paul and Nehemiah, but I don't think it will work for me. You need to know this: If the Spirit of God is alive in you, if God is renewing your attitude and actions in Christ Jesus, if you are falling more and more in love with Jesus every day, then you are an example worth following. People can follow you as you follow Christ. So what do you show them? Show them your walk with Christ. Show them how you relate to God. Show them how you live out your faith through your day-to-day life. Take responsibility for other's growth. Some people call this discipleship. I call it spiritual leadership.

A high school buddy of mine taught me this lesson early in my walk with Jesus. His name is Chris Seay. When I met Chris, he wasn't one of the leading pastors for emerging generations as he is today. He was just a high school kid with a passion for Christ and a desire to see God work in our school. He led a small Bible study and prayer group. This was a serious prayer group.

Paul founded the church at Corinth himself, as recorded in Acts 18. The congregation in the city of Corinth was a mixed one, with both Jews and non-Jews comprising the multi-ethnic congregation. Both 1 and 2 Corinthians deal with issues of spiritual leadership, an issue which had divided the Corinthian church.

They prayed not only for their needs but they also prayed, by name, for people they knew who didn't know Christ. I was one of those people.

Just after I prayed to receive Christ, Chris invited me into a relationship that shaped my life forever: "Mikey, now that you know Christ, let me help you follow Him." I quickly accepted his invitation because I knew absolutely nothing about my new faith. Over the next few months, through this relationship, I learned how to pray, study my Bible, and relate to others in Christ-honoring ways. He taught me a ton in a short amount of time, but the lasting lesson from our relationship is that spiritual leaders invite others into their lives. They lead in an up-close and personal way. They lead by example.

### THE YOUNG LEADER

These first few principles are for everybody. We can all lead with more prayer, more commitment, and more investment in others. But there are also some principles we can learn from Nehemiah that are specific to young leaders.

**What are some of the challenges that young leaders face?**

**What about the advantages?**

We don't have to shrink back from leading as young adults. Our leadership ability is more about who we are than it is about how old we are. Catch this in Nehemiah 7:1-2:

> **"When the wall had been rebuilt and I had the doors installed, the gatekeepers, singers, and Levites were appointed. Then I put my brother Hanani in charge of Jerusalem, along with Hananiah, commander of the fortress, because he was a faithful man who feared God more than most."**

Listen to the audio file "Nehemiah Expanded I," more teaching from author Mike Hurt about the practical implications of Nehemiah. Your group leader will send it to you via e-mail.

It was Hanani who first brought the news of Jerusalem's plight to Nehemiah. Hanani inspired his brother to take on the building project of his life. This wasn't why Nehemiah trusted his brother with so much responsibility in Jerusalem, though. This was no under-the-table nepotism act either. No, Nehemiah saw something more than just his brother when he saw Hanani. He saw a man of integrity who feared God more than most people did. This is typical Nehemiah. He led with integrity and feared God, so it was a no-brainer to trust another person with those same qualities to lead the city he had just rebuilt. That person just happened to be his brother.

One of the verses that has marked my life since the day I read it is 1 Timothy 4:12: "No one should despise your youth; instead, you should be an example to the believers in speech, in conduct, in love, in faith, in purity." Paul wrote this to a young minister named Timothy. He also wrote it to every young adult who wants to make a difference for Christ. I am so encouraged by this verse because it means that our leadership potential isn't determined by our age; it's determined by our character. It's more about who you are than how old you are. It's more about your experience with Christ than it is your experience in leadership.

Some young leaders are offended by this verse. *Why do we need God's Word to affirm our youth?* they ask. Not me. I need this verse. I'm typically one of the youngest leaders in the circles of leadership that I run in. God has consistently put me in places of influence that don't necessarily match up with my age. This pattern started months after I came to know Christ and hasn't stopped yet. Being the youngest in the room and being in charge can be kind of intimidating. Questions race through your mind like: *Will anyone follow? Do I know how to lead? If I ran out of the room screaming, would anyone notice?*

That's when I learned a secret. If I set an example worth following, people will follow no matter how old I am or they are. If people see godliness in me, then they will follow. I also learned that people don't expect me to have all of the answers. Instead, they are trusting me to turn to God for wisdom and direction. They aren't just looking to me. They are looking to God in me. When they see Him, they will follow me.

It's a liberating truth. It's also a permission-giving truth. This verse gives us all freedom to lead in the ways that God has called us to lead no matter our age. We don't need to wait until we "grow up" to lead. In fact, many of the modern heroes of the faith were young leaders:

Paul probably met Timothy on his first missionary journey when he visited Lystra. Later, Timothy accompanied Paul, Silas, and Luke on Paul's second missionary journey (Acts 16:1-5). Timothy was a comparatively young man, and Paul thought of him as a trusted coworker and was as close to him as a father.

Adoniram Judson was born in 1788 and was an American Baptist missionary who labored for almost 40 years in Burma (now known as Myanmar). He was the first Protestant missionary sent from North America to preach in Burma. His mission and work led to the formation of the first Baptist association in America, inspired many Americans to become or support missionaries, translated the Bible into Burmese, and established a number of Baptist churches in Burma.

- Adoniram Judson was 25 when he began his missionary work in Burma.
- Dwight L. Moody was 23 when he started what would become the largest Sunday School of its day.
- William Carey was 31 when he published, *An Enquiry into the Obligations of Christians to Use Means for the Conversion of the Heathens,* his classic work on missionary activity.
- Mother Teresa was 18 when she received her calling to serve the poor in India.
- Martin Luther was 34 when he tacked the 95 Thesis on the doors of the Castle Church.

Sometimes when I think of men and women of this stature, I forget all that they did when they were young because all of the pictures I see of them aren't exactly glamour shots from their youth. But make no mistake about it, these were young leaders who changed the world.

> Are these stories of young leaders intimidating or encouraging to you? Why?

## STEP UP TO LEAD

This is one of the places where the church needs to wake up: Trust young adults to lead. Often, if you are young and ready to lead, you only have two options—you can take care of the babies in the nursery or you can go on the next youth retreat. If God has called you to this, then great, but what if God has called you to a ministry that doesn't involve diapers, bottles, and lights out battles? What do you do? Odds are you suck it up and do what the church needs because you want to serve and make a difference. But the church loses every time this happens, because young leaders need to lead in more ways than simply filling an empty ministry slot.

Something special happens when young leaders lead. I have seen it time and time again. When young leaders lead, the energy level and excitement in the church grows. Not only do young leaders bring energy—they also bring innovation. Part of this is because we're so insecure about our skills. Because of that insecurity, we spend our time doing everything we can to learn how to lead; innovation occurs as a result of that learning. The true source of the innovation is a young leader's willingness to apply their unique abilities to a ministry setting.

We have different skills, experiences, and technical abilities than the generations before us. When we creatively apply our uniqueness, innovation is the result. When we lead, other young leaders will also step up to lead. When a young leader sees one of their peers leading in a significant way, they will step up to do the same. If your church is struggling with young leaders, then take the initiative. Step up and lead. Make a high-energy, innovation-driven difference, and watch God bring others alongside of you. It will happen.

**Can you identify a specific area in your church community where leadership is needed?**

**What do you think the Lord wants you to do about it?**

## LEARN AS YOU LEAD

The second lesson that you and I—as young adults—need to learn from Nehemiah on spiritual leadership is this: If you can't submit, you can't lead. This is a tough truth. We are eager, easily excitable, and in our minds, ready to lead *now*. The challenge is that God is the Judge of readiness—not us. And His measuring stick is often far different from ours. God wants us to be eager to serve. He wants us to be excited about what He has called us to do. But what He wants even more than these things is for us to be ultimately submitted to Him and His leadership.

*Outreach* is an organization that prizes innovation in church ministry. They annually highlight, both on the Web and in their magazine, exceptionally innovative churches and individuals. For more information, check out *outreach.com*.

*"Submit to every human institution because of the Lord, whether to the Emperor as the supreme authority, or to governors as those sent out by him to punish those who do evil and to praise those who do good. For it is God's will that you, by doing good, silence the ignorance of foolish people"* (1 Peter 2:13-15).

This submission is expressed not only in our relationship with Him, but in our relationships with the leaders God has put in place in our lives. I have seen young leaders struggle with this many times. They get the "you're not the boss of me" syndrome. Rather than submitting to the leadership of others, I've seen young leaders rebel against the leadership of those in authority. Often, they blame it on generational differences. You hear things like, "They just don't know what it takes to reach the next generation."

Young leaders may also grab for power or authority too quickly or in sinful ways. This one is especially troubling. That impulsion reveals what we believe about God's sovereignty. If we really believe that God raises men and women to leadership, then why would we use ungodly or sinful tactics to gain leadership positions for ourselves?

As young leaders, we should strive to learn the discipline of submitting to the leaders around us, and Nehemiah shows us how. Remember, Nehemiah was a cupbearer before he was a governor. He was a trusted wine taster before he was the rebuilder of Jerusalem. He learned how to submit to leadership and trust his leaders before God put him in a position of leadership himself. He helps us see how to get our leadership lives in the right order. Too many times, I think we get this backward. We look for God to give us a position. We look for God to put us in a great place so that we can show how we trust Him in great ways. We look for a way for God to honor us rather than a way for us to honor Him by honoring those in authority.

Nehemiah turned this thinking on its head. He looked to honor God. He was more interested in his calling to love God with his entire life than in his position. He submitted himself to God and trusted Him for the rest. This is the strongest foundation from which he could lead.

Even when Nehemiah knew that God was calling him back to Jerusalem to rebuild the city, he submitted to King Artaxerxes' leadership. Here is the scene:

> **"During the month of Nisan in the twentieth year of King Artaxerxes, when wine was set before him, I took the wine and gave it to the king. I had never been sad in his presence, so the king said to me, 'Why are you sad, when you aren't sick? This is nothing but sadness of heart.' I was overwhelmed with fear and replied to the king, 'May the king live forever! Why should I not be sad when the city where my ancestors are buried lies in ruins and its gates have been destroyed by fire?' Then the**

The Hebrew word translated *sad* literally means "bad," so in a way, the king asked Nehemiah, "Why do you look so bad?" There was a certain danger in revealing feelings in the presence of the king since to appear anything less than happy in the king's presence could be interpreted as having disloyal thoughts about him.

**king asked me, 'What is your request?' So I prayed to the God of heaven and answered the king, 'If it pleases the king, and if your servant has found favor with you, send me to Judah and to the city where my ancestors are buried, so that I may rebuild it'" (Nehemiah 2:1-5).**

I love the humility he demonstrated here. It had been around three Jewish calendar months since he heard the news of Jerusalem's state. He came before the king to serve him. Did you catch that? He didn't come to make a demand or to call the king to action. *He came to serve.* In so doing, the king noticed Nehemiah's condition and put it perfectly—Nehemiah was experiencing true "sadness of heart" (Nehemiah 2:2). Even with the king's expression of concern, Nehemiah didn't come off too strong. He humbly told the king about Jerusalem. The king quickly took it to the next level with his question, "What is it that you want?" Nehemiah's response was a quick prayer to God. Here he stood before the king who was essentially offering his trusted servant all of his resources, but rather than just looking to the king, he looked to God and then spoke. He asked to go and rebuild the city.

As you're building your leadership foundation, apply the lessons we learn from Nehemiah. Worry more about your devotion than about your position. Look to submit before you look to lead. Honor the leaders above and around you as an expression of your submission to God. In doing so, you will show that you may be young according to the calendar but you are maturing at the core.

Leadership isn't just about achieving a certain position or holding a prestigious title; it's about the day-to-day life choices we make and taking hold of the opportunities God gives us to lead from wherever we are. That's leadership reimagined.

Read the digging deeper articles called "The Cast," "Time Line (overview)," and "Nehemiah's Time Line" to enrich your understanding of the biblical text. Your group leader will e-mail them to you as you prepare for this week's discussion.

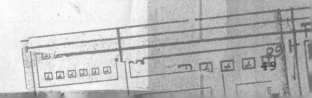

# Session Two - Building Blocks

## Read

* Day 1     Nehemiah 3:20-32
* Day 2     Nehemiah 4:1-14
* Day 3     Nehemiah 4:15-23
* Day 4     Nehemiah 5:1-13
* Day 5     Nehemiah 5:14-19

## Memorize

"No one should despise your youth;
instead, you should be an example to the
believers in speech, in conduct, in love,
in faith, in purity" (1 Timothy 4:12).

## Challenge

There's work to be done. There are leaders
who need to emerge. Spend some time looking
around your own faith community. What are
the needs in your own church? Where can you
passionately use your gifts and talents? Seek
out someone in leadership and ask about the
possibility of either leading in ministry or
faithfully volunteering to follow. Step up to
the challenge.

notes

notes

The work is progressing. Walls are
getting higher at a remarkable pace.
But what is more amazing is the spirit of
the people. It's like they have something
to believe in again. It's like they have
hope. They are beginning to see—we are
beginning to see—past ourselves. We are a
part of something bigger than us. And we
are coming together accordingly.

I met more people for the first time
today. There is a great family that is
working hard together on the eastern
section. What attracted them to me
was the father working alongside his
children. Even the little ones, who
couldn't really do much, were carrying
pebbles to put down by their father.
I worked beside them for a good while,
and they have a remarkable story.
These people who chose the hard road
of returning to Jerusalem amaze me.
They said they were honored I worked
beside them; I assured them the feeling
was mutual.

Perhaps this project is about more than the physical structure we are building. It must be so. You cannot escape this feeling of togetherness that has infiltrated our city. God bless these people. They are not my builders . . . they are my friends.

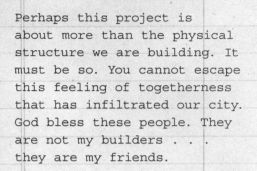

upper 9th ward Habitat Build, New Orleans, LA

## COMMUNITY REDISCOVERED

The story sounds unbelievable. Fifty-two days simply isn't enough time to accomplish what they did. Fifty-two days—that's less than two months. That's half a football season. It's not even a full season of the year. And yet there they were—Nehemiah and his wall-builders—at the end of those comparatively few days, standing on top of what they had constructed.

When we read a book like Nehemiah, we may fall prey to a little "not in my backyard" syndrome. Typically, this type of thought happens when something or someone unfavorable moves into the neighborhood. You hear people say it time and time again when a bar, strip club, or something else not conducive for family starts to encroach their territory: not in my backyard. Though the expression usually refers to something bad moving in, we often have the same mentality about the work of God.

Though it's rarely stated publicly, much of the church suffers from "not in my backyard" thoughts when it considers the miraculous. We read Scripture and we see God do incredible things, but we don't really believe it can happen in our backyard. We hear of stories from around the globe of how God is reaching more and more people with the gospel, but we don't expect to see it happen around us. We see God answer the prayers of others, but we continue to pray without confidence. It's not that we don't want God to work among us; we just don't think He will.

> **Why do you think we have trouble believing God will do the miraculous?**

> **Is it possible for us to position ourselves to see a greater move of God? How?**

Mark Buchanan would argue that our view of God limits what can be accomplished in and through us. He spells this out in great detail in his book *Your God Is Too Safe*. Consider picking up a copy.

Don't fall into the temptation of unbelief when you study the community God was building in Nehemiah's day. Make no mistake—while the people might have thought they were building walls—God knew they were building a lot more than that. As the bricks, stone, and mortar went together, God was rebuilding a community that had been decimated by sin, disappointment, and despair. You might say that the walls were being repurposed—no longer would the structure be exclusively about safety and protection; the walls would also be a consistent reminder to the people of who they were and what God had done and was continuing to do in their midst. The same thing can happen today.

Don't let yourself wonder if you could have done what they did. You could. Don't let yourself think that somehow the people of Nehemiah's day are so different than you and me. They're not. Don't let yourself wonder if you could accomplish the impossible if God called. You can.

Here's proof: Look again at the cast of characters we see in Nehemiah. They are ordinary people—sons, daughters, moms, dads, leaders, followers, craftsmen, and farmers. And they were all being led by a cupbearer! Do they sound like a finely tuned team who could rebuild Jerusalem's walls in 52 days? Probably not. They sound more like the type of people who you and I live, work, and play with every day. They sound like us.

## GET "NEXT TO HIM"

So what made their community so dynamic? What allowed them to accomplish more in two months than many communities of faith accomplish in a lifetime? The answer is found in Nehemiah 3. The phrase "next to him" is used eight times to describe who was responsible for repairing certain sections of the wall. "Next to him" refers to far more than the location of the people, though. The three words showed how people from all over Jerusalem came together to do what none of them could do alone. Together they found the strength of biblical community.

This "next to him" thinking repurposed their relationships. These repurposed relationships changed the world, and the pride of Jerusalem was restored as the wall grew from rubble. These relationships provided security and safety against opposition as families became protectors of community. These relationships provided for one another's needs both through the giving of the tithe and through forgiving of debts. We also see that these relationships provided the context for spiritual growth and commitment.

Mike Hurt, author of *Repurposed*, is dedicated to the development of biblical community. One of the most effective ways to do this is through small groups. For more tips and tools from Mike, visit *smallgroupresources.org*.

This is the type of community you and I need in our lives. We need to be part of a fully devoted, ever-committed group of people who are sold out to each other and to God's purposes. We need the safety and security that true community provides. We need people who have our backs. We need people who will play key roles in our own spiritual growth.

While this is the type of community we all need and most of us want, sadly it isn't the type of community we experience on a day-to-day basis. Instead of finding deep, lasting relationships, we find ourselves in the midst of inconsistent connections with others. Instead of feeling safe and secure in community, we wonder who can be trusted. Instead of finding communities committed to spiritual development, we find churches and groups committed to almost everything except authentic, powerful life change.

*"Carry one another's burdens; in this way you will fulfill the law of Christ" (Galatians 6:2).*

As a result of these realities, even with our strong desire to connect with others, we live very disconnected lives. The good news is that this can change. Our relationships can be revolutionized just as we read about in Nehemiah's day, especially if we apply what we learn from their involvement in community.

> If we desire this kind of community, why do you think so many of us still live disconnected lives?

> Do you feel like you value spiritual privacy more than spiritual community? Why or why not?

For the church to be all that God has called it to be, we need to pick up some of the "next to him" thinking we see in Nehemiah. To begin with, we need to understand that the church is first and foremost a relational environment. We are more than just a group of individuals or people with common interests and values. We are a family. Our relationships are central to what God wants to achieve in you and me through His church.

I love the way that Cloud and Townsend put it in their book, *How People Grow* They argue that God, at some point, did not throw up His hands in exasperation and say, "Study, prayer and other disciplines aren't working so I guess that I will have to use people to spur on other people's spiritual growth." The church is not God's plan B for our spiritual growth; people are God's plan A for spiritual growth. God wants to use the people He has put in your life to accomplish His purposes. This is "next to him" theology.

**Who are the top five people you believe God has put in your life to accomplish His purposes?**

Read the digging deeper article called "The Purpose and Life Situation of Nehemiah," to enrich your understanding of the biblical text. Your group leader will e-mail it to you as you prepare for this week's discussion.

**How can you move "next to them"?**

The first step to engaging in biblical community is to see who God has put next to you. This was the wall-builders' first point of connection—taking a look to each side to see who else was holding rocks. So who has God put in your life? Connect with them, be committed to one another, and see what God does next. Often, though, it's not quite that easy, because "next to him" connections fly in the face of some of our thinking regarding who we should be in community with. We gravitate naturally toward people who are like us—the ones who look like us, sound like us, earn like us, and think like us.

We most often choose to connect to people who are our age and in our life stage because it seems easy, natural, and right. While there's a lot of value in connecting with people like you, if your community doesn't branch beyond that, you are severely limiting your perspective. The life experiences, and God experiences, of people older, younger, richer, poorer, darker, and lighter than you can serve to broaden your perspective of God and faith in general. God has put people in our lives for a reason, and He expects us to connect to them even if it doesn't make complete sense to us.

Trust that God can turn a group of strangers into a group who feels like family. In 2 Samuel 23:8-17, we see how "next to him" thinking worked for David. This is the passage where we learn about David's mighty men. As these men are introduced, they are linked with the phrase "next to him." When you read about them, these guys seemed more at home in street fights than they did in committed relationships, yet together they were David's mighty men.

They were so committed to their leader and trusted each other so much that they were willing to risk life and limb just to get David a drink of water from the gate of Bethlehem. David cared deeply for them as well. When he realized the great risk they took because of a flippant comment he made, he couldn't bear drinking the water they brought to him. This "next to him" thinking is a very powerful bond.

## THE GIVING AND GETTING

As we enter into community, we need to view it through two lenses. We need to look at it through the lens of what we get, and we need to look at it through the lens of what we give. Clear vision through both lenses is absolutely essential to experiencing biblical community.

If you close your "what I give" eye, you become a consumer of community. You may enjoy it, but no one else will enjoy you. If you close your "what I get" lens, you become one who lives just outside of community. You meet others' needs, but you don't allow others to meet yours. You contribute to another's growth, but you don't allow others to contribute to you. You experience "fish bowl" community. As you sit on the outside of the bowl, you witness a beautifully created ecosystem. You witness the beauty of

Read more about the accomplishments of David's mighty men in 2 Samuel 23 and 1 Chronicles 11.

community, but you never get wet. You are simply a witness of God's activity and not a true participant.

In the Book of Nehemiah, you find a relational road map for both what we should give and get in community. Through Nehemiah's life and leadership, we see both are required. We also see that it's possible to both meet the needs of others and have your needs met through community. Some of us need to face the fact that we are a bit jaded when it comes to our confidence in the church. We've been disappointed one too many times to trust. We've been burned one too many times to try again. We've taken care of others while our needs have been ignored. It's a sad state in the church when we can be so young and so jaded.

**Are you more prone to give or get from your church experience? Why?**

**What are some ways you can start to balance your giving and receiving?**

At the 2006 Desiring God Conference, speakers like Tim Keller, Mark Driscoll, and John Piper discussed, among other things, church consumerism. For the audio recordings of their talks you can visit *desiringgod.org/ events/NationalConferences/ Archives.*

As you study Nehemiah, I ask you to let your guard down. Look with your spiritual eyes and see God's design for biblical community. Also look and see the people who God has put around you. Look and see all that God wants for you. Now, let's look at what you go through as you connect to community.

## GETTING BIGGER

The first thing we get when we are part of a biblical community is the reminder that we're part of something bigger than ourselves. One of the inaccuracies of the modern church is the idea of a personal relationship with Jesus. But our relationship with Jesus isn't an exclusively personal one. Hear me out before you close the book and call me a heretic. Jesus died for everyone—not just for you. Many people have prayed to receive Christ—not just you. God wants everyone to know His Son—not just you. God has a plan for everyone—not just you. Seen in that light, we realize that Jesus isn't my *personal* Savior; He's the Savior of the people of God, of which I am one. Your relationship with God is not all about you.

This lesson is quickly learned in community. It's in community that we learn the lesson of God's common work among His church. It's in community that we learn that God intimately cares for each of us equally. It's in community that we learn we're part of something far bigger than ourselves. It's in community that we whisper the prayer, "God, be big in my life. Use me for Your purpose. Use me as a part of Your church, which is far bigger than me."

One of the perks of living in D.C. is the opportunity to do some once in a lifetime things. One of those things for me and my family was a visit with the president on the South Lawn of the White House. A visit to the White House is no small deal. There are required security clearances that must be obtained weeks in advance. There is even a dress code. Coats and ties are encouraged. Jeans and flip flops are outlawed.

As I was getting dressed for our visit, I looked at my wife and jokingly told her that this may be my last day at home for awhile. She was game, so she asked why. I told her that when I met the president and shook his hand he would immediately ask me to step into a high-level position to help him solve some of the world's problems. I told her I was certain he would instantly recognize my leadership ability and would have no option but to ask me to join his team.

I have to think this is part of what people felt like when they were around Nehemiah. He had a tendency to call people to do things that they wouldn't normally do on their own accord. Housewives put down their pots and picked up tools. Kids put down their toys and picked up rocks to rebuild the city's walls. Men put down the tools of their trade, picked up swords, and worked together. In a heartbeat their lives were radically altered because of Nehemiah's leadership.

Have you ever experienced anything similar? What's one thing you would never have done without the encouragement of your community?

Through our experiences in biblical community, we should be hearing the same call to be active participants in something far larger than ourselves. We should be looking for the ever-present opportunity to join God in His activity around us. We should encourage each other to listen for God's call and answer with our obedience. In doing so, we'll become the type of community described by Spurgeon: "Every person to his post, everyone of you to your weapon during this day of battle. For God and for His truth, for God and for what's right—let every one of us who knows the Lord seek to fight under His banner!"[14]

## GETTING CLOSER

In relationships with others, we also find a place to grow in our love for God. Through biblical community, we enter into relationships where spiritual growth isn't optional. Interestingly enough, though, spiritual growth and commitment isn't necessarily required either. It seems that when a group of people start living life together as God intended, with Him as their focus, the natural result is a closer walk with Jesus and greater commitment to Him and each other. We see this in one of my favorite chapters of Nehemiah.

In Nehemiah 8, we see how the people of Jerusalem responded when the Word of God and the worship of God was returned to their city. Their worship experience started at sunrise with Ezra opening up the book of the Law. He climbed atop a wooden platform and read from it praising God from sunrise to noon. As Ezra stood above the crowd, the people bowed down and worshiped the Lord. Along with Ezra, the Levites instructed the people. This is the type of Bible study that I want to be a part of and the type of Bible study that we all need in our lives:

Charles Haddon Spurgeon was England's best-known preacher for most of the second half of the 19th century. In 1854, just four years after his conversion, Spurgeon, then only 20, became pastor of London's famed New Park Street Church. The congregation quickly outgrew their building, moved to Exeter Hall, then to Surrey Music Hall. In these venues Spurgeon frequently preached to audiences numbering more than 10,000—all in the days before electronic amplification.

**"They read the book of the law of God, translating and giving the meaning so that the people could understand what was read" (Nehemiah 8:8).**

As the people understood what was being read, they didn't do what you and I do when we begin to understand things. They didn't take notes or underline passages in their Bibles. They didn't ask insightful questions to show their wisdom and knowledge. They responded with weeping and mourning, so much so that Nehemiah had to address the crowd:

> **"Nehemiah the governor, Ezra the priest and scribe, and the Levites who were instructing the people said to all of them, 'This day is holy to the LORD your God. Do not mourn or weep.' For all the people were weeping as they heard the words of the law. Then he said to them, 'Go and eat what is rich, drink what is sweet, and send portions to those who have nothing prepared, since today is holy to our LORD. Do not grieve, because your strength comes from rejoicing in the LORD'" (Nehemiah 8:9-10).**

Have you ever been a part of a spontaneous experience like this?

What do you think keeps things like this from happening more frequently?

Oh, how I wish that there would be more of this in the community you and I experience. We need the Word of God to be central to our gatherings. We need the type of conviction that leads to confession. We don't need someone else's opinion on things. We need a word from God. We aren't coming together for therapy. We are coming together to study the Bible in such a way that we can understand and apply it to our lives. And we need to celebrate everything we have together in Christ.

This happens when we make spiritual growth and an understanding of God our primary motives for connecting in community. Too many times we let the secondary elements of community become primary. We advertise food and fun, but if we're not careful, those elements become the limit of our relationships. We get really good at casuality in community and consequently, these unintentional relationships never do anything to further our spiritual growth and development. What people want and need isn't another activity to add to the calendar. What we want and need is an environment in which we can grow.

The good news is that we can follow the pattern here. Once we have a powerful experience with God, we can go celebrate that and enjoy each other along with choice food and sweet drinks. Just be careful not to get it backwards as you build community. Never put food, fun, or fellowship in front of spiritual growth. Never put the secondary above the primary.

Before we move on, I want to make one additional warning. This may seem obvious, but it must be said: Don't let your love for spiritual growth or spiritual disciplines outshine your love for God. Remember, loving God is the desired outcome of study and discipline. Andrew Murray puts it this way:

> "Even the most sincere and committed Christian faces a danger: it is the danger of substituting prayer and Bible study for living fellowship with God. Your desire to pray earnestly and diligently may so occupy you that the light of his countenance and the joy of His love cannot enter you. Your Bible study may so interest you and intrigue you that, yes, the very Word of God may become a substitute for God Himself. These pursuits can hinder fellowship because they keep the mind, heart, and soul occupied instead of leading you into the presence of God."[15]

If you find yourself guilty of doing the right things in the wrong ways as Murray describes, confess it and ask God to help your love for Him grow as you connect to community.

"If there be any of you who by [private confession of our sins to God] cannot quiet his own conscience, but requires further comfort or counsel, let him come to me or to some other [Christian] of God's word, and open his grief" (*The Book of Common Prayer*).

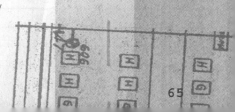

How has connection to community spurred you to spiritual growth?

How high on your relational priority list is the spiritual development of those around you?

Listen to "A New Day Dawns" by Through a Glass from the *Repurposed* playlist. Your group leader can send you the playlist via e-mail, or you can download it at *threadsmedia.com/media.*

## GETTING AUTHENTIC

In community, we also find a safe place to be real. In Nehemiah 9, we read of another not so typical worship experience. This type of worship experience isn't the kind of thing you would hear about at modern church leadership conferences or seminars. It's certainly not an experience you would find on a week-to-week basis inside a church building on any given Sunday:

**"While they stood in their places, they read from the book of the law of the LORD their God for a fourth of the day and spent another fourth of the day in confession and worship of the LORD their God" (Nehemiah 9:3).**

Confession of this sort is a missing ingredient in today's experience of biblical community. When was the last time you were a part of a gathering where confession of sin occurred out loud, in the open, and for an extended period of time? When was the last time that God's Word was taught in such a way that confession of sin was the only natural response?

Right now you may be thinking, *This type of communal confession of sin is an Old Testament thing. God doesn't want that from us as New Testament Christians because in Christ we are completely forgiven.* That statement is only half right. In Christ, you and I are completely forgiven, but that doesn't revoke the need for the confession of sin both public and private:

> **"Therefore, confess your sins to one another and pray for one another, so that you may be healed. The intense prayer of the righteous is very powerful" (James 5:16).**

It's not that God withholds forgiveness based on our confession; He doesn't. Notice that James says confession leads to healing. We confess to one another so we can remind each other of the forgiveness God has given to us in Christ. The forgiveness comes from Him, but the reminder of that forgiveness comes from each other.

Not only is confession good for the soul, but it's also good for your prayer life. Too many times in community we ask people to pray for the things in our lives we *want* them to pray for instead of praying for the things we *need* them to pray for. That is to say, we ask them to pray for the element in our lives we are most comfortable with—the sale of a house, the sickness of a relative, for our aunt's uncle's cousin's dog. We pray for the easy things and avoid the rough requests. Do you want the people who love you the most praying for your wants or for your needs? If you desire the latter, practice the discipline of confession in community.

What benefit of connecting to community do you need the most right now? Why?

What steps can you take inside your community to try and move it to be an environment where needs like yours can be met?

Listen to the audio file "Nehemiah Expanded II," more teaching from author Mike Hurt about the practical implications of Nehemiah. Your group leader will send it to you via e-mail.

## GIVING SERVICE

Now that we have looked at a few of the benefits of connecting to and receiving from our community, we need to look at what each of us should be contributing to the communities we are a part of. Remember, we must give *and* receive in community.

The early church father, Justin Martyr, wrote in *Apology* about the situation in Acts 4: "We who valued above all things the acquisition of wealth and possessions, now bring what we have to a common stock, and communicate to every one in need."

The first thing we contribute to community is a commitment to serving one another. Service should be a natural part and outpouring of our life together in community. Many times people enter into community hoping that their needs will be met. They will make friends. They will have things to do. They will learn more about Scripture. They will get whatever they want. We need to turn this thinking on its head. We should connect to see how we can serve. We should connect to see how we can meet the needs of another first instead of seeking to meet our own needs. We should connect to see how we can contribute to the group rather than always looking for what we will take away from the group.

The funny thing is that when we start to live by this standard, our needs do get met because everyone is serving someone else instead of serving themselves. Think about it—if each of us is looking to meet the needs of others, then all of our needs will be met. That's how it worked in the context of the first century church:

> **"Now the multitude of those who believed were of one heart and soul, and no one said that any of his possessions was his own, but instead they held everything in common. And with great power the apostles were giving testimony to the resurrection of the Lord Jesus, and great grace was on all of them. For there was not a needy person among them, because all those who owned lands or houses sold them, brought the proceeds of the things that were sold, and laid them at the apostles' feet. This was then distributed to each person as anyone had a need"** (Acts 4:32-35).

This wasn't your standard Sunday School class or small group. This was serious community. These people understood what it meant to give all they could to serve one another.

## GIVING PEACE

Authenticity has been trumpeted by our generation for years. We've said we want our church experiences to be real. We don't want plastered on smiles and "praise the Lords." We want genuine relationships with one another. Authenticity isn't all that it's advertised to be, though. Real people have real problems with one another. Nehemiah, who dare I say was as "real" as anyone you will meet, had real conflict with people. He experienced conflict with some inside the city walls and many outside the city walls.

We also show our commitment to community through how, when, and why we resolve conflict. Romans 12 teaches that as far as it is possible, as far as it depends on you, live at peace with everyone. Our faith makes us responsible—not necessarily *for* everyone—but we are responsible *to* everyone. Healthy relationships matter to God and should matter to us. We should take the condition of our relationships very seriously.

The apostle Paul said, "If possible," and not only that, but also "on your part, live at peace with everyone" (Romans 12:18). He puts the responsibility squarely on your shoulders. There's always an option for peace in our relationships. To show your commitment to community, work proactively through every conflict situation.

The key to all of this—both what we get and what we give in community—is taking responsibility for our connection to community. We can't wait around for community to happen to us. We must be intentional about the environments we are involved in. It's your choice how deeply you give and how deeply you receive. Remember God wants you to be involved in both. This give and take relationship with those around us is what life together is all about.

If you are in the middle of a rift right now, take the first steps as far as it depends on you. Take a step toward peace. First, pray for the situation. Ask God to show you your role and the best steps for you to take. Then, at a minimum, commit in your heart to live in a peaceful way toward the person with whom you're in conflict. Take it a step further and give them a call or write them a note. Maybe you even need to talk one-on-one to restore the relationship.

# Session Three - Building Blocks

## Read

* Day 1     Nehemiah 6:1-9
* Day 2     Nehemiah 6:10-19
* Day 3     Nehemiah 7:1-60
* Day 4     Nehemiah 7:61-73
* Day 5     Nehemiah 8:1-12

## Memorize

"Now the multitude of those who believed
were of one heart and soul, and no one
said that any of his possessions was his
own, but instead they held everything in
common. And with great power the apostles
were giving testimony to the resurrection
of the Lord Jesus, and great grace was on
all of them" (Acts 4:32-33).

notes

## Challenge

Too often we drift through life, making no intentional relationships. Instead, we gravitate toward people who look like us, think like us, and just happen to be in our path. Start being intentional this week. Gather together a small group of people committed to seeing each other grow spiritually. Set up some parameters for this group of spiritual encouragement (When will you meet? What will you talk about? What will you expect of each other?). Try and have some variety in your group in terms of age, race, and economic status.

notes

SESSION THREE   REPURPOSED

upper 9th ward Habitat build, New Orleans, LA

The people are hungry. With no end in sight to the famine, difficult decisions must be made. It pains me to think we have come so far and yet still we sit on the edge of failure. We must press on. But in our pressing on, we must not put the project ahead of the needs of the people.

How is it that we have come so far and yet there are still those who insist on their personal welfare and comfort at the expense of their countrymen? I suppose in any society there are the rich and there are the poor; I must do what I can to help those with plenty see the evil in taking advantage of those in want. We must care for each other.

Will there ever be a community that truly cares for the lowly? Will there ever be a people who give so freely that no one goes to sleep hungry?

I must confront this issue. I have done what I can out of my own pocket, but others must do the same. I will not avoid the wrongdoers; I will call them out and trust God to do the rest. If they refuse to give of their grain freely, then surely all our efforts at rebuilding this city and these people will crumble before our eyes. People will abandon their posts so their families can eat. God has brought us to this point; if it is His will for our journey to end here, so be it. I cannot believe, however, that He will not act again on our behalf . . .

## COMPASSION RENEWED

One of the recurring themes throughout Nehemiah's life is that he was a man whose passion for God influenced every part of who he was. His passion resulted in compassion in action.

We see this epitomized in Nehemiah 5. In this passage, we find many of the same issues that have emerged to the forefront of our conscience. Like Nehemiah, we have become aware of issues of injustice in today's world. Throughout the world people struggle with extreme poverty. Others grapple with ever-increasing debt. Many more are sold into slavery when they cannot repay their loans. We see people straining under the weight of societal and structural inequities:

> **"There was a widespread outcry from the people and their wives against their Jewish countrymen. Some were saying, 'We, our sons, and our daughters are numerous. Let us eat grain so that we can eat and live'" (Nehemiah 5:1-2).**

Here's the scene: There was not enough food in Jerusalem to sustain all the needs of the people. I imagine that the supplies of the city looked like grocery store shelves just before a big snowstorm or hurricane—everything's gone unless, of course, you can sustain life on ketchup and toothpaste. Large families, in particular, were feeling the pressure. Something had to be done. They either needed grain brought to them or they would have to go and get it. And if the people had to leave and get food, the walls would be unprotected. Nehemiah's enemies were chomping at the bit waiting for such a chance to undo the work that had been done to repair the walls.

> **"Others were saying, 'We are mortgaging our fields, vineyards, and homes to get grain during the famine'" (Nehemiah 5:3).**

Some solved one problem by creating another. They mortgaged their livelihoods and homes to get grain. So I guess it's safe to assume the famine wasn't affecting everyone. Someone had to have grain to sell if people were able to purchase it. It's also likely that those with grain for sale were selling it at such a high rate that the only purchase option was to buy it on credit. The gap between the "haves" and the "have-nots" was just as big then as it is today.

The wealthiest nation on earth has the widest gap between rich and poor of any industrialized nation. The combined wealth of the world's 200 richest people hit $1 trillion in 1999; the combined incomes of the 582 million people living in the 43 least developed countries is $146 billion (*globalissues.org*).

> **"Still others were saying, 'We have borrowed money to pay the king's tax on our fields and vineyards. We and our children are just like our countrymen and their children, yet we are subjecting our sons and daughters to slavery. Some of our daughters are already enslaved, but we are powerless because our fields and vineyards belong to others'"** (Nehemiah 5:4-5).

There were a couple of things at play in this last group of people. First was the issue of the king's tax. The people of Jerusalem, along with the rest of the known world, were required to pay taxes to King Artaxerxes. Apparently, these taxes were so extensive that people had to borrow money from others to pay them. If you have ever had to pay your income taxes on a credit card, you know exactly what these people were facing. This leads us to the second issue—Jews were loaning money and charging interest to their own countrymen. While this might not sound like a big deal to you and me, this profit-making venture was in direct opposition to the Law:

> **"Do not charge your brother interest on money, food, or anything that can earn interest. You may charge a foreigner interest, but you must not charge your brother interest, so that the LORD your God may bless you in everything you do in the land you are entering to possess"** (Deuteronomy 23:19-20).

Why do you think God cared so much about His people charging one another interest?

At its peak, the Persian Empire stretched from the Indus River across the Near East to the eastern Mediterranean coast, south into Egypt along the Nile River to Sudan, across Anatolia, and into Thrace and Macedonia. All subjects were required to pay taxes for the benefit of the empire.

How does this principle relate to us today?

## TIME FOR ACTION

God wanted there to be no doubt about His people's love for one another. Many financial advisors warn against loaning money to friends and family because of the stress it puts on relationships. Deuteronomy isn't necessarily advocating loaning money to those closest to you; it is, however, saying that as you loan each other money, don't enslave one another in debt by charging interest.

In his book on Nehemiah, Chuck Swindoll writes, "No Jew was ever to enslave another Jew. Such action was evidence of an absence of love and concern for his brother . . . God's instructions (which they willfully disobeyed) would have protected and preserved the Jews in Nehemiah's day during this period of stress. But because they chose their own problem-solving method, they sank into the quicksand of increasing compromise."[16]

> What does the way you treat the people around you reveal about your relationship with God?

Chuck Swindoll is renowned for his books portraying biblical characters in an intensely personal way. His book about Nehemiah, *Hand Me Another Brick*, is no exception.

If you, too, are looking for a way to channel your compassion, check out *coolpeoplecare.org,* which offers a daily suggestion of compassionate action, in many cases, specific to your community.

Compromise and a lack of concern for the needs of others were two things that Nehemiah couldn't stand by and simply watch. His biblical compassion drove him to action. Notice what he did first:

> **"I became extremely angry when I heard their outcry and these complaints. After seriously considering the matter, I accused the nobles and officials . . ." (Nehemiah 5:6-7).**

He got mad, and he put together a plan. I think we wrongly assume that compassionate people are all smiles, and intense feelings like frustration, resentment, and anger aren't a part of their emotional vocabulary. But compassion isn't always friendly. We also see that compassion is much more than unrestrained rage. So Nehemiah pondered. He took a moment and thought, *Given how I am feeling, how can I best meet the needs of the people?*

Have you ever experienced a moment like this? What did you do?

## AMEN

Once he formulated his plan, he called together the nobles and officials and he confronted the issues of usury head on. This meeting wasn't about building a coalition to see how the needs of the people could be met. It wasn't a meeting to talk about an optional interest-release program to help people deal with the famine and the credit crunch. Nehemiah didn't shrink back. He didn't withhold the truth:

> " . . . I accused the nobles and officials, saying to them, 'Each of you is charging his countrymen interest.' So I called a large assembly against them and said, 'We have done our best to buy back our Jewish countrymen who were sold to foreigners, but now you sell your own countrymen, and we have to buy them back.' They remained silent and could not say a word" (Nehemiah 5:7-8).

Did you catch their response to his accusations? There were no excuses. There were no "yeah buts." There was silence. I guess it's hard to argue with the truth. With the power people in the palms of his hands, Nehemiah continued:

> "What you are doing isn't right. Shouldn't you walk in the fear of our God and not invite the reproach of our foreign enemies? Even I, as well as my brothers and my servants, have been lending them money and grain. Please, let us stop charging this interest. Return their fields, vineyards, olive groves, and houses to them immediately, along with the percentage of the money, grain, new wine, and olive oil that you have been assessing them" (Nehemiah 5:9-11).

As you know, this was more than just a call to financial integrity among Jewish brothers and sisters. Nehemiah was calling them to obey God's Word: "You can loan money to one another, just don't charge interest. Make no one your slave." The people responded.

The word *amen* has become little more than a way of saying "good-bye" to God at the end of a prayer. Its origin, however, reveals a much more significant use. *Amen* actually means "I agree," or "may it be so." It is a statement recognizing the truth of what has been said, and the one who says it declares their support and dedication to the statement.

**"'We will return these things and require nothing more from them. We will do as you say.' So I summoned the priests and made everyone take an oath to do this. I also shook the folds of my robe and said, 'May God likewise shake from His house and property everyone who doesn't keep this promise. May he be shaken out and have nothing!' The whole assembly said, 'Amen,' and they praised the LORD. Then the people did as they had promised" (Nehemiah 5:12-13).**

Does the people's response surprise you? Why?

I don't know about you, but I can't remember the last time I was reprimanded for doing something wrong and responded like these people did. Essentially, they said thanks to Nehemiah, and then they worshiped God together. Even though they had just lost a significant revenue stream, they weren't bitter or angry, and I think I know why—Nehemiah had just taught them a lesson on biblical compassion, and they fully embraced it.

*"Do nothing out of rivalry or conceit, but in humility consider others as more important than yourselves" (Philippians 2:3).*

Do you know the difference between compassion and biblical compassion? Random House defines *compassion* as "a feeling of deep sympathy and sorrow for another who is stricken by misfortune, accompanied by a strong desire to alleviate the suffering."[17] By this definition, *compassion* is a combination of feeling and activity. This definition is good but incomplete when compared to biblical compassion. Biblical compassion is a heart-felt attachment to the needs of others and heart-felt action to meet that need *based on the character of God*.

Learning to live with biblical compassion will revolutionize the way you see the world around you. No longer can you simply live for your own desires. You are responsible for the world around you. No longer can you notice a need and simply sit back and let it go unmet. You are responsible to the people around you. No longer can your love for people be limited to a mission trip, a service project, or a program through your church. You begin to see real-time needs of people around you most everywhere you go. Your heart begins to reformat itself, and consistent expressions of God's love and kindness are the result.

**Why do you think it's essential for compassion to be based on the character of God?**

**Why do you think so many of us struggle with maintaining consistent biblical compassion?**

Shane Claiborne, author and activist, lives in the middle of urban Philadelphia among the poor and homeless population of the city. You can read more about Shane and his view of compassion and the church's role in changing the world at *thesimpleway.org.*

## HEART CHECK

The church today should be teaching and modeling God-centered, biblical compassion just as Nehemiah did. The church should be in the lead when it comes to producing compassionate followers who are committed to meeting the needs of the world around us. The church shouldn't come in second place to star-driven campaigns or flash in the pan causes. The church shouldn't primarily look to meet its own needs. Based on what we know of God and based on what we know of the world around us, the time has come for the church to act with God-centered, biblical compassion.

For the church to take this step, we must learn about the heart of our Heavenly Father. Remember, biblical compassion starts with the heart of God—not with the needs of man. We must understand that compassion is at the core of God's character. Don't miss Jesus' response to the needs of His world:

Read the digging deeper articles called "The King's Cupbearer," and "Ancient Gates" to enrich your understanding of the biblical text. Your group leader will e-mail them to you as you prepare for this week's discussion.

**"Then Jesus went to all the towns and villages, teaching in their synagogues, preaching the good news of the kingdom, and healing every disease and every sickness. When He saw the crowds, He felt compassion for them, because they were weary and worn out, like sheep without a shepherd. Then He said to His disciples, 'The harvest is abundant, but the workers are few. Therefore, pray to the Lord of the harvest to send out workers into His harvest'" (Matthew 9:35-38).**

In this passage we see the heart of the Father expressed perfectly by His Son. We see Jesus expressing the compassion of God by teaching and healing people of their disease and sickness. Rather than being impressed by the crowds He was drawing, He was impressed by the great needs of others. Our lesson doesn't stop there. We also see God's desire for all His children to engage in acts of compassion to those in need. I can imagine Jesus' tear-filled eyes as He commanded His disciples to pray for more workers to enter the harvest field.

Understanding the condition of our Heavenly Father's heart should lead us to analyze the condition of our own hearts. I learned this lesson for myself a few years back. My dad was driving home from playing golf one Sunday afternoon just as he had done many times before. This day was different though, because as he drove, blood stopped flowing through his heart causing it to explode in his chest. His car went from side-to-side on the road, eventually coming to rest in a field. Despite the heroic measures of some medically trained bystanders, he died that day.

I'm not typically a hypochondriac, but for the next six months, every time I walked up stairs or across a parking lot, I would feel my chest tighten and my heart race. I was like Fred Samford from the old TV show *Samford and Son:* "This is the big one!" I was certain that I had issues with my heart.

I went to the doctor multiple times to figure it out. Each time I went to the doctor, the conversation went something like this: "Doc, I'm dying here. I know that I am only 23, but here's my history. My dad passed away from a heart attack six months ago and my mom is just about to undergo triple bypass surgery." The doctor would then argue with me saying that I was perfectly healthy and that I didn't need any tests. Even with his advice, I went back time and time again. I knew the condition of my dad's heart and I wasn't going to let my heart go unchecked.

Finally, the doctor relented and ordered a couple of tests. The first was a stress test. They hooked me up to an EKG and put me on a treadmill. Perhaps a stress test isn't the best time to step on a treadmill for the first time, but that's what I did. I did my best to get through seven hard minutes. At the end, to my amazement, the technician said, "You look great. You are fine."

The next test was an echocardiogram. For this test, they laid me on an exam table, rubbed cold gel on my chest and then used a sonogram to check how my heart was functioning. As I watched blood pump through my heart on the display screen, I kept thinking, this is bad news. I see a problem. The tech disagreed. At the end of the test, I was given a clean bill of health.

The doctor was right all along. I was perfectly healthy. My heart was fine. Even though I felt a little silly for pressing so hard for the tests, I was glad I did. I knew the condition of my heart. I knew how my heart compared to my father's.

> **Based on what you are learning from Nehemiah and based on what you know of our Heavenly Father's heart, I have to ask: What is the condition of your heart when it comes to responding to the world around you with compassion?**

International Justice Mission is a human rights agency that secures justice for victims of slavery, sexual exploitation, and other forms of violent oppression. For more information and to get involved, visit *ijm.org*.

## MORE THAN A CAUSE?

We are the first generation to have instant access to tragedies around the globe. We are also the first generation to have been bombarded with images of the poor and needy since we were young. None of us can say we don't know about the great needs in the world. Even with all of this information on hand, some of us have not developed a sense of compassion for the world around us. Instead, we've chosen to have calloused, apathetic hearts beating in our chests. In many ways, we have hearts of stone. If this is you, you need to know that your heart beats in opposition with the Lord's. You can't disconnect your relationship with those in need from your relationship with God. It's entirely inconsistent to say you love the Lord while you do nothing to stand up for those in need.

Once we honestly reflect on the condition of our heart, we need to notice the needs of the people around us. Many in the church today see the needs of others—especially on a global level. We are growing worldwide in our concern regarding AIDS. The fact that more than 25 million people are afflicted with AIDS in Sub-Saharan Africa is beginning to gain the church's attention.[18]

Issues regarding social injustice are becoming front-burner topics to the evangelical community as a result of compassion-based ministries such as International Justice Mission led by Gary Haugen. These are good things, but we can't exclusively focus on the high-profile pleas for help. We don't just need to notice the needs around the globe; we need to notice the needs of those in our own city, state, and country. If we ignore the needs of the people nearest to us, then we miss God's immediate call on our lives.

**Are there any particular needs of others that you get fired up about and want to do everything you can to meet?**

**If the answer is none, how can you position yourself to encounter those in need more readily?**

We also need to consider the very real possibility that our compassion might be rooted in concern for ourselves rather than others. Do we really care about others or do we want to be a part of what appears to be the next big trend for church? Take AIDS in Sub-Saharan Africa for instance. Will our awareness of the devastation caused by AIDS cause us to actively meet the needs of people in countries such as India (largest number of people living with AIDS outside of South Africa), Vietnam, and Thailand (where AIDS is the leading cause of death)?[19]

If our answer to this question is *yes*, our concern over the AIDS crisis will spread beyond Africa, and we'll back up those words with action. If our answer is that our concern is centered on Africa, then it's possible we care about AIDS because it's cool to do so. If that's the case, we aren't becoming compassionate Christ-followers; we are only part of a trend, and we're simply filling another church program. Get this: *Compassion is not a program of the church. It is an act of the church.*

Now it's time to move from sympathy to action. Many in the church today notice the needs of others and feel badly about their condition, but don't act on their feelings. They respond with sympathy rather than compassion. Sadly, the institutional church is in part to blame for much of this.

Over the years, the church has outsourced its compassion-based ministries. Just as the globalization of corporations has greatly affected the U.S. economy, the outsourcing of compassion-based ministries has devastated the church's caring economy. It happens as we send missionaries across oceans. It happens as we start parachurch organizations to love college students or those who are incarcerated. It happens as we send money to local food kitchens and homeless outreaches. With each of these well-intentioned ministries, the message to the people of God from the institutional church, intentional or not, is this: Caring for those in need is someone else's job. Compassion is no longer something we look for in our own lives; we look for it in someone else's ministry. Compassion is just another service we pay for.

**What are some excuses you have used to avoid meeting the needs of others?**

According to *until.org*, more than 22 million people have died from AIDS worldwide. Another 42 million live with HIV/AIDS. By the year 2010, five countries (Ethiopia, Nigeria, China, India, and Russia) with 40 percent of the world's population will add 50 to 75 million infected people to the worldwide pool of HIV.

Why do you think God is so concerned that you are physically involved in meeting the needs of others?

How is that experience different than writing a check?

## CALLED AND EQUIPPED

We find ourselves in a very similar position as the disciples in Matthew 14. We see a need and think someone else should meet it:

The disciples had a good argument in Matthew 14. They had all just returned from intense mission trips, and they were all tired. Jesus, however, refused to let them rest.

> **"When Jesus heard about it, He withdrew from there by boat to a remote place to be alone. When the crowds heard this, they followed Him on foot from the towns. As He stepped ashore, He saw a huge crowd, felt compassion for them, and healed their sick. When evening came, the disciples approached Him and said, 'This place is a wilderness, and it is already late. Send the crowds away so they can go into the villages and buy food for themselves'" (Matthew 14:13-15).**

Do you see the disciples' reaction here? By their logic, they had no part to play in meeting these people's needs. "Send the people away," they urged. They saw the need, but they wanted no part in solving it. Feeding the people was someone else's job. Jesus had a different idea though. He had compassion on them. Next came one of the most miraculous stories in the entire Bible—Jesus fed a crowd of thousands with someone's lunch.

These guys didn't get what it means to have biblical compassion: "Jesus, what do we have that can meet these needs?" They saw the need, but they didn't respond with actions that mirrored the heart of Christ. It's my opinion that these guys had everything they needed to solve the problem for that multitude. They had everything they needed, except they were frozen with one question. It's the same question that paralyzes many of us into inaction: "What in the world can I do to solve a problem that's so much bigger than me?"

The disciples had the resources they needed to make a difference, and so do we. They had the physical Christ. We have the promise that Christ is with us in the Person of the Holy Spirit, even until the very end of the age. They had the teaching of Jesus on the hillside, calling people to new levels of devotion, forgiveness, and healing like never before. As Christ-followers, we have the story of God in our hearts, lives, and mouths when we speak it. The disciples had untapped potential. We have untapped potential in the spiritual gifts that God has given us. God has given every Christ-follower supernatural abilities to go out and meet needs we never thought possible. Given who we are in Christ, we have everything we need.

It's critically important to realize God has called and equipped all of us to respond to the people around us with biblical compassion. Don't miss the opportunity to express the care and character of God. Nehemiah could have simply ignored the needs of the people. He could have demanded that they simply return to work and finish the task, but he didn't. He took the time to not only notice the need, but take action and meet the need in a God-honoring way. In doing so, he taught the people of Jerusalem to not only love God but how they could love each other in very practical ways.

That's biblical compassion. It's more than a feeling. And it's more than statements like, "Somebody ought to do something about this problem." It's action, and it's action rooted in the heart of God. It's action motivated by the belief that God has put us on this earth to make a difference, to be a blessing to other people, and to live out the prayer of Jesus that the will of God would come to pass on earth as it does in heaven.

Listen to "O The Deep Deep Love" by The Blackthorn Project from the *Repurposed* playlist. Your group leader can send you the playlist via e-mail, or you can download it at *threadsmedia.com/media*.

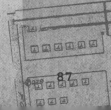

# Session Four - Building Blocks

## Read

* Day 1        Nehemiah 8:13-18
* Day 2        Nehemiah 9:1-15
* Day 3        Nehemiah 9:16-38
* Day 4        Nehemiah 10:1-29
* Day 5        Nehemiah 10:30-39

## Memorize

"If a brother or sister is without clothes and lacks daily food, and one of you says to them, 'Go in peace, keep warm, and eat well,' but you don't give them what the body needs, what good is it? In the same way faith, if it doesn't have works, is dead by itself" (James 2:15-17).

## Challenge

You were challenged this week to commit yourself
to biblical compassion, action for the good of
another rooted in the heart of God. So get started.
Start looking for ways to be involved in the lives
of others. If you need some help getting started, check
to see what your local church is doing in
the community, or try these sites:

* *coolpeoplecare.org*
* *ijm.org*
* *voa.org*
* *namb.net/dr*
* *habitat.org*

notes

notes

I've had the most curious revelations during this experience. In fact, it seems that somehow, through all the building, confrontation, shared meals, dashed hopes, and everything else that has happened to us, the presence of my God has remained faithful. No, not just faithful; His presence has increased.

But that's not right either; surely God is present at all times in all places. Perhaps instead my recognition of His presence has increased.

I have begun to realize He is everywhere, and that awareness has heightened my spiritual senses. No longer do I simply inspect the work, eat a meal, go to sleep, or have a conversation; every moment seems to be holier now. It is as if all these moments that once were so ordinary have a certain weight about them now, almost as if they are heavy. God has always been present in these mundane moments, these inconsequential periods, these menial tasks, but I have overlooked Him until now. No more.

My God, help me to remember the holiness of the moments, that there are no small times, people, conversations, or tasks. Help me to approach my day with the knowledge of Your abiding presence, being fully convinced that You care deeply about the small as well as the large.

upper 9th ward Habitat Build, New Orleans, LA

## WORK REPURPOSED

In his book *Dedication and Leadership*, Douglas Hyde tells the story of an extraordinary sermon he heard on Easter Sunday 1948 in a church on the edge of a Southeast Asian jungle. The old Indian priest, while preaching to a group of mainly poor peasants, told the story of the women coming to find Jesus on the first Easter Sunday. When they arrived, they looked in the garden. He wasn't there. They looked in the tomb. He wasn't there. Then he said, "You don't have to look around the garden to find the risen Lord. He is in your hands. When you go out to work tomorrow, whether you are riding a trishaw, or digging a drain, or whatever you are doing as your daily work, you will be cooperating in God's work of creation. God is in your hands."[20]

As the preacher said this, an old man sitting in his congregation began to look at his "toil-worn, calloused, twisted hands, and broken nails almost in awe." As he stared at his hands, a great truth entered his heart. His work would never be the same. Now, no matter how degrading his manual labor might be, it would be meaningful for him. His Christianity suddenly became relevant to his work. To put it another way, his work was now relevant to his faith.

While I'm not sure about the old Indian preacher's theology when it comes to God being in our hands, I am sure that the lesson learned through his message is one that we must all apply to our lives. Our faith and our work are to be married. We must resist the urge to divorce our work from our belief. We have become very good at living much of our lives separate from our faith. There's no better example of this than our work lives.

Somehow, who we are and what we believe on Sunday sometimes has little impact on what we do for a living. We affirm God's truth on Sunday, and yet we practice shady business. We strive to be servant leaders at church, but we are cutthroat at the office. We commit to make God our top priority when challenged in a worship service, but when the rubber meets the road our schedules tell a far different tale of our ultimate focus. We find ourselves worshiping our jobs, positions, and paychecks during the week and God on Sundays.

**Why do you think many live such segmented lives?**

Douglas Hyde was the news editor of the London Daily Worker, a Communist newspaper. Hyde was a member of the Communist party for 20 years before renouncing the party and becoming a Christ-follower.

How does the idea of a fully integrated spiritual life relate to Jesus' statement in Matthew 22:37-38?

What would a "fully integrated life" look like if you were living it?

Through our study of Nehemiah, we'll see a far different perspective on work and faith. Nehemiah was a man who lived a fully integrated life, meaning his faith influenced every part of who he was. He decided at some point to make God's perspective his first priority in every situation. He knew who he was working for. Because of this, he saw everything he did as worship to God. He removed the barrier between the secular and sacred. Everything he put his hands to was a God thing.

Read the digging deeper articles called "What Nehemiah Saw," and "Nehemiah Inspects Jerusalem's Walls" to enrich your understanding of the biblical text. Your group leader will e-mail them to you as you prepare for this week's discussion.

## WHO'S THE BOSS?

Nehemiah exhibited working for the Lord when he was the governor of Jerusalem:

> **"Furthermore, from the day King Artaxerxes appointed me to be their governor in the land of Judah—from the twentieth year until his thirty-second year, 12 years—I and my associates never ate from the food allotted to the governor. The governors who preceded me had heavily burdened the people, taking food and wine from them, as well as a pound of silver. Their subordinates also oppressed the people, but I didn't do this, because of the fear of God. Instead, I devoted myself to the construction of the wall, and all my subordinates were gathered there for the work.**

**We didn't buy any land. There were 150 Jews and officials, as well as guests from the surrounding nations at my table. Each day, one ox, six choice sheep, and some fowl were prepared for me. An abundance of all kinds of wine was provided every 10 days. But I didn't demand the food allotted to the governor, because the burden on the people was so heavy. Remember me favorably, my God, for all that I have done for this people"** (Nehemiah 5:14-19).

For the entire 12 years, Nehemiah received no money for serving as the governor of Jerusalem. He could have followed the example of previous governors by taking almost a pound of silver plus food and drink. Basically, he could have had a pile of money plus the finest in basic provisions. Instead of bilking the people and lording his position over them, he opened his home. He footed the bill. He gladly accepted the burden of leadership.

Nehemiah did this because of his reverence for God. I love how he contrasted his actions to those of the previous governors and their assistants. They were all about their position and power. Nehemiah was all about serving the people and serving God. He was different and he knew it.

That begs the question: Is your life, work ethic, and ambition any different than the people around you? Can you confidently contrast your life to the lives of those who don't follow Christ, or are you a part of the "whatever-it-takes," cutthroat culture prevalent in society?

Your answers to these questions are a good indicator of your level of belief in God's sovereignty and control over your life. It is God who puts us in the positions that we have. God raises some women up and puts some men down. Our positions are God's business, not ours. Nehemiah knew this so he was able to trust God and lead in a way that showed evidence of that trust. He was able to do as Peter would later command:

**"Shepherd God's flock among you, not overseeing out of compulsion but freely, according to God's will; not for the money but eagerly; not lording it over those entrusted to you, but being examples to the flock. And when the chief Shepherd appears, you will receive the unfading crown of glory"** (1 Peter 5:2-4).

Listen to the audio file "Nehemiah Expanded III," more teaching from author Mike Hurt about the practical implications of Nehemiah. Your group leader will send it to you via e-mail.

Nehemiah knew that ultimately he wasn't a cupbearer. He wasn't a governor. He wasn't a builder. Ultimately, Nehemiah was convinced that regardless of is position, he was working for the Lord.

Get this: No matter your profession, if you are a Christ-follower you are working for the Lord. Learning this truth will revolutionize your life. It will forever change the way you answer the following questions:

What do you do?

Who do you work for?

The answer to the first question will be based on what you do in your day-to-day job. Some of us may be doctors. Others may be attorneys. Some may be craftsmen. Others may be high-tech gurus. These positions are based on God's call on our lives, our education, and our desires at the time of our call. The answer to the second question isn't about what you do, but it is nevertheless a decision you make either consciously or subconsciously. If you've made the decision to give God your life, then you work for the Lord. We all have the same boss if we know Jesus. He is the CEO of our lives. He is the one who provides our paychecks. He is the one who provides our promotions. He is our boss.

Unfortunately, most of us are unwilling to recognize Jesus' authority over our lives. I see this time and time again in Washington. People seem to find their status in the name of their bosses. People who work on Capitol Hill do it. People who work for high-powered consultant firms do it. People who work at

**R**

For a classic work on discovering the spirituality of every moment, pick up a copy of *Practicing the Presence of God* by Brother Lawrence.

cutting edge tech firms do it. Even people like me, who work at large churches, do it. We find our status in the wrong place. We serve the wrong boss.

**Where are you finding your status?**

**Why do you think you find it there?**

To call Jesus *Lord* had a much greater significance in days past than now. In the New Testament, *kurios* or *Lord* means master or owner. When applied to Christ, the word corresponds to *Jehovah*, implying God's supreme power over the universe.

When we serve the right boss, we learn that our work is never in vain. Whether we work as a politician or a garbage collector, a teacher or a pastor, we work for the Lord. If you feel as though your current job is beneath you, your work is not in vain. If you don't like the people you work with or for, your work is not in vain. If you have big time dreams and a small time job, your work is not in vain. We never work in vain because we are really working for the Lord—even in our entry-level, underpaying, boss-hating jobs. Pastor Steven Furtick calls this the principle of representation:

> "The principle of representation states that when you serve someone else in the name of the Lord, for the glory of God, the person that you are serving becomes a representation of Jesus Christ. And even if that person doesn't appropriately appreciate you, acknowledge you, or compensate you, your labor is never in vain . . . God is the ultimate destination of all of your investments."[21]

The next time you're feeling like you're working in vain, take a moment and remember who you are really working for. Do what Nehemiah did in Nehemiah 5:19. Ask God to remember you for what you are doing. As you do this, don't be shy. Admit how hard things are. Confess your struggle. Then ask God for His favor, just as Nehemiah did. But realize, too, that God's favor comes in a variety of flavors. Some days it will be what you and I consider to be behind-the-scenes blessings like having endurance, displaying a good mood, or accepting our roles. Thank God for these "favors" and His work inside of us. Other days, the favor of God may come in a very public way. These are blessings of success, a great idea, or a completed project. Keep your eyes open to God's favor on your work life, and then you'll know your work is never in vain.

**What are some other ways God shows His favor?**

**What are some of the ways that you can recognize the favor of God in your work life?**

> "Whatever you do, do it enthusiastically, as something done for the Lord and not for men, knowing that you will receive the reward of an inheritance from the Lord—you serve the Lord Christ" (Colossians 3:23-24).

## WORK REDEEMED

Once we know who we are working for, we begin to see our work in a different light. This is important because I believe we all, deep inside of us, long for work to be something more than just work. To fully understand why, we need to return to the garden of Eden. One of the consequences of Adam and Eve's sin—and our sin for that matter—is that the word *toil* entered our vocabulary, and the sweat of the brow became a requirement to eat. Because of sin, work became work. No longer were days filled with walking through the ultimate farmer's market. Their supply of fruits, vegetables, and proteins dried up. Since that time, the fields have yielded a harvest of thorns and thistles, and crops have required sweat-filled days to produce (Genesis 3:17-19).

Can you relate? I know I can. But I also know that just as Jesus has overcome every other consequence of the fall, He has overcome this as well. If you and I are in Christ, then we are all new. We are totally redeemed, and we are totally usable by God in every area of our lives. Know this: If God has redeemed you, He wants to use you to honor Him. This is how He redeems even our work—God tears the veil between secular and sacred. If we are working with godly purposes and godly practices, even the most secular job becomes sacred.

Nehemiah knew this. As we have studied before, we know that Nehemiah's call to rebuild the wall came from an intense time of prayer and fasting before the Lord. Notice how a seemingly secular job of rebuilding a wall became a God thing for Nehemiah:

> **"So I said to them, 'You see the trouble we are in. Jerusalem lies in ruins and its gates have been burned down. Come, let's rebuild Jerusalem's wall, so that we will no longer be a disgrace.' I told them how the gracious hand of my God had been on me, and what the king had said to me" (Nehemiah 2:17-18).**

Nehemiah had a life-altering passion to build a wall because he knew that by constructing a wall, so much more could be accomplished. He knew the city of Jerusalem and the worship of God would be reestablished through this task. He also knew it was God who called him to the task.

**What tasks are you convinced that God has called you to?**

God's call to the task is an essential element to seeing the sacred in the most secular of tasks. It is God who gives purpose to the task, because in every task there are God-given ministry opportunities along the way. Did you notice that Nehemiah didn't spell out all that was coming to the people in the coming weeks and years as a result of their work? He didn't outline all of the reforms he would institute. He didn't describe the worship experiences they would engage in. He didn't tell everyone how the walls were going to be repurposed to be an enduring symbol of their renewal. He simply started with the wall and took every God-given opportunity that followed.

This should be our goal as well. Start with what God has put in your hands. Do the job that God has given you. See this as your calling from God, and then take every opportunity that He gives you to extend His love and work to those around you. By doing so, you'll see your work and worship sync as you expect God to work in both areas.

## THE UNCOMPARTMENTALIZED LIFE

As you do this, you will be overcoming one of the major sins of the modern church: extreme compartmentalization. We have church friends. We have church books. We even have church clothes. That's a funny one. What distinguishes church clothes from our everyday clothes? Nothing. Do we have some special clothes that bring us favor with God? Absolutely not. Does God want us to dress our best on Sunday and dress however we want every other day? Nope. God cares how we dress every day.

I love the T-shirt in simple block letters that reads, "These *are* my church clothes." It is both theologically correct and fashionable. If you are like me and you weren't raised in the church, the idea of "church clothes" may be a little foreign to you. I had never heard of church clothes until I was preparing to graduate from eighth grade.

The school administration sent home a letter outlining what was to happen on this grand occasion. Among other instructions, we were told to wear church clothes. At the time, I was confused because I wasn't sure why it mattered what type of clothes we wore under our graduation gowns. I also didn't have a clue what church clothes were.

After I began my faith walk, I quickly learned that church clothes meant ironed khakis and a polo shirt. It was like a uniform. Even though Dockers had no part in my everyday life, they were an essential element every Sunday. As I look back at it, I quickly and subconsciously learned how to compartmentalize my life.

It happened with my music, too. After accepting Christ, I did away with all of the music I listened to before I knew Christ. I trashed my CDs. I reset my radio stations. Top 40 and rock were replaced by the local Christian station. In

Listen to "Fear and Faith" by Michael Olson from the *Repurposed* playlist. Your group leader can send you the playlist via e-mail, or you can download it at *threadsmedia.com/media.*

fact, I put the Christian station on all five of my radio presets. I went out and bought all of the Christian CDs I could afford.

Why did I do all of this? Did I have sin issues with music in the past? No, music had never been a huge part of my life. Did Christian music help me worship God more consistently? Maybe. But the real reason that I made the musical switch was because someone told me all secular music was bad. Everything about every secular song was evil, and it would lead to bad things in my life.

If someone told me that now, I would be better prepared to reply. First of all, not every secular song is evil. Some are, but not all. Some are completely inappropriate for the ears and mind of one who knows Christ. We should avoid those songs littered with vulgarity or charged with sexual overtones, but that's because God's Word commands us to avoid these things—not because the songs are secular.

But I would also challenge someone committed to a "Christian music only" standard to examine his or her life to see whether the rest of their lives measure up. Does he only visit Christian Web sites? Does she only watch Christian newscasts? Does he only watch Christian TV? Does she live in a completely Christian bubble?

**In what ways are you guilty of compartmentalizing your life?**

An honest conversation through these issues would show that it's not possible to live in a Christian bubble. We cannot compartmentalize our lives nearly as much as we want to. We can't separate ourselves nearly as much as we desire. We can't, and we should thank God we can't. We should thank God, because anyone who watches only Christian TV, for instance, would have some significant issues, including whacked doctrine, some really bad hairstyle role models, and a very unfortunate desire to purchase gold-plated furniture.

Instead of striving to compartmentalize our lives, we should strive to find continuity. We should strive for consistent beliefs and actions no matter the situation we're in. We should be living lives of integrity before God and before men so that in all things God gets the honor and the credit for all that is happening in our lives.

What obstacles do you face in your work life to spiritual integration?

## MORE THAN A JOB

In regard to work, Dan Miller provides a unique perspective on how we can achieve this by outlining the difference between a vocation, a career, and a job. The starting point in this discussion is our vocation. Our vocation is our calling. It's what we are doing that adds both meaning to our lives and makes a difference in the world around us. These types of callings stay consistent over time. Our careers, on the other hand, don't. Careers are a particular line of work. Our career provides a basic framework for how we are living out our vocation. Careers may change frequently, but not as frequently as our jobs.

This is why many of us—even just a few years out of college—aren't doing anything closely related to our degrees. We're doing jobs to bring home paychecks. If you're an average worker, you'll have somewhere between 14 to 16 jobs in your lifetime.[22]

So what do we need to learn from this? Our purpose doesn't come from our job. How can it if we're going to have 15 different jobs before everything is said and done? Also, our jobs need to be more than just a source of income. They need to add to our calling. Each job needs to be part of a career path that supports what God wants from our lives. It's also important to seek to understand our careers in light of God's call on our lives. This discussion is often minimized to whether or not someone is called into "full-time" vocational ministry. That's a huge mistake.

R

Dan Miller is the president of The Business Source, a company specializing in creative thinking for personal and business development. In books like *48 Days to the Work You Love*, Miller tries to help people find a job in which work links up with passion (*48days.com*).

We are all called to ministry. Everyone needs to ask the question: *Is my career helping me achieve what God wants from me?* Be careful as you ask it though, because it's a life-changing question. I have much respect for people who have asked this question and taken risky steps of faith to enter into a career that's more in line with their calling.

Lawyers become teachers. Teachers become social workers. Nurses become doctors. In order to make these moves with confidence, you must know your calling or vocation, which only comes from God. Friends and coworkers can advise you, but the level of conviction that you'll need to live out your calling only comes from God. This calling, when prioritized, will shape every aspect of your life.

What was Nehemiah's calling? Don't be too quick to answer this one. If you do, you might be tempted to say his calling was to rebuild Jerusalem. His calling was deeper than that:

> **"Please, Lord, let Your ear be attentive to the prayer of Your servant and to that of Your servants who delight to revere Your name" (Nehemiah 1:11).**

I believe Nehemiah's calling was to *revere*—to regard with awe, deference, and devotion—God's name. This calling fed every other role Nehemiah fulfilled in his life. His career path was one of significant leadership positions. He used his influence at every level in ways that were totally congruent with his calling. Consider his various jobs: cupbearer, construction manager, political reformer, national guard, religious reformer, and governor. In each of these roles, he showed his reverence for God's name and sought to defend the name of God at every turn.

**What is your calling?**

According to the Westminster Shorter Catechism, the actions forbidden by the third of the Ten Commandments are as follows: "The third commandment forbiddeth all profaning or abusing of anything whereby God maketh himself known."

How do you see that calling relating to your career?

It's not always as easy for us as it seemingly was for Nehemiah. Sometimes we struggle to integrate our lives, but the lessons we learn from Nehemiah are of the utmost importance. Think about it—odds are if you're struggling with your calling, then you're struggling at work. You are probably also struggling with compartmentalizing your faith.

But the struggle itself is a sign of hope because it means you are dissatisfied with a "church clothes" segmented life. Without merging your work and your worship, you'll never find your true 24/7 calling. Nehemiah spent days on his face before the Lord to confirm his calling. You can do the same. If you're struggling, come before the Lord. Ask for wisdom, boldness, and the courage to act on what He reveals to you.

Christ-followers must come to the point where they recognize that there are no ordinary moments. There are no non-spiritual times. Your cubicle is a holy place, just as your church building is, because in God's economy, you are the temple of the Holy Spirit. Wherever you go, there He is. And whatever moment you enter into, God is there too. If we can begin to see our lives through the lens of Christ, we will realize that the compartmentalization of our days, weeks, and years simply does not make sense. And we'll realize that each second is a time to put our hands to the work of God in the world.

Nehemiah did. He understood that building the walls was more than a construction project. He came to believe that God was intensely interested in the seemingly ordinary day-to-day lives of seemingly ordinary people. He came to believe that God wanted to repurpose everything we do, to move it from the secular to the sacred, from the mundane to the holy. God can do the same for us, if we are willing to let Him.

Do you have the opportunity to do what you do best every day?

Chances are, you don't. All too often, our natural talents go untapped. *Strengths Finder 2.0* by Tom Rath is a book/Web-based program to help you discover how to maximize your talents. For more information, check out *strengthsfinder.com*.

# Session Five - Building Blocks

## Read

* Day 1    Nehemiah 11:1-21
* Day 2    Nehemiah 11:22-36
* Day 3    Nehemiah 12:1-26
* Day 4    Nehemiah 12:27-47
* Day 5    Nehemiah 13:1-31

## Memorize

"Whatever you do, do it enthusiastically,
as something done for the Lord and not
for men, knowing that you will receive the
reward of an inheritance from the Lord—you
serve the Lord Christ" (Colossians 3:23-24).

## Challenge

To reinforce the idea of God's presence in your work, pick up a copy of the short work by Brother Lawrence called *Practicing the Presence of God*. It won't take you long to read, but the benefit will last a lifetime.

notes

notes

# ENDNOTES

## SESSION 1

1. Meredith Eller, *Beginnings of the Christian Religion: A Guide to the History and Literature of Judaism and Christianity* (Lanham: Rowman & Littlefield Publishers, Inc., 1955), 162.
2. *The Eerdmans Bible Dictionary,* ed. David Noel Freedman (Grand Rapids: Eerdmans, William B. Publishing Company, 2000), 756.
3. *The Interpreter's Bible,* ed. George Arthur Buttrick (Nashville: Abingdon Press, 1954), 662.
4. Jim Collins, *Good to Great: Why Some Companies Make the Leap . . . and Others Don't* (New York: HarperCollins Publishers, 2001), 20.
5. Ibid., 22.
6. *jimcollins.com/lab/level5/p2.html*
7. Ibid., *Eerdmans Bible Dictionary,* 362.
8. Ken Hemphill, *The Antioch Effect: 8 Characteristics of Highly Effective Churches* (Nashville: Broadman & Holman, 1994), 132.
9. John Ortberg, *Everybody's Normal Till You Get to Know Them* (Grand Rapids: Zondervan, 2003), 36.

## SESSION 2

10. Bill Hybels, 2006 Leadership Summit Message, 2006.
11. Andrew Murray, *The Best of Andrew Murray on Prayer,* Ed Elliott (compiler), (Urichsville: Barbour Publishing, 1998), 121.
12. J.I. Packer, *Knowing God* (Downers Grove: InterVarsity Press, 1993), 101.
13. "Thou Shalt Know Thy Big Mac," *Relevant,* Jan/Feb 2008, 20.

## SESSION 3

14. Charles Haddon Spurgeon, *The Best of Charles Spurgeon,* ed. Stephen W. Sorenson (Colorado Springs: Honor Books, 2005), 13.
15. Ibid., *The Best of Andrew Murray,* 123.

## SESSION 4

16. Charles R. Swindoll, *Hand Me Another Brick* (Nashville: Thomas Nelson, 1998), 103.
17. "Compassion," *Dictionary.com Unabridged* (v 1.1) Based on the Random House Unabridged Dictionary, © Random House, Inc. 2006. Available from: *http://dictionary.reference.com/browse/compassion.*
18. George Ochoa and Melina Corey, *The 100 Best Trends, 2006: Emerging Developments You Can't Afford to Ignore* (Avon: Adams Media Corporation, 2005), 61.
19. Ibid., *The 100 Best Trends 2006,* 61.

## SESSION 5

20. Douglas Hyde, *Dedication and Leadership* (Notre Dame: University of Notre Dame Press, 1966), 96.
21. *stevenfurtick.com/personal-development/the-principle-of-representation/*
22. Dan Miller, "My Job, My Calling: Can They Be The Same?" Christian Placements Newsletter, January 21, 2008.

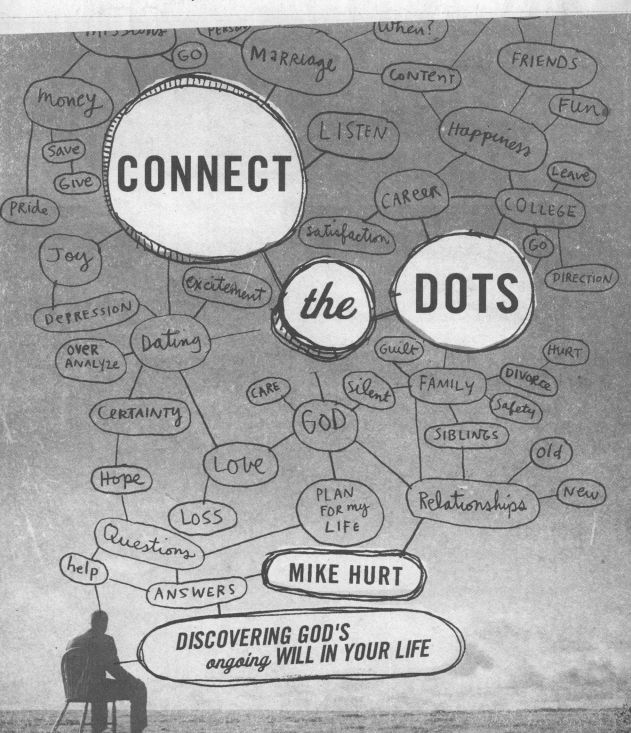

# TABLE of CONTENTS

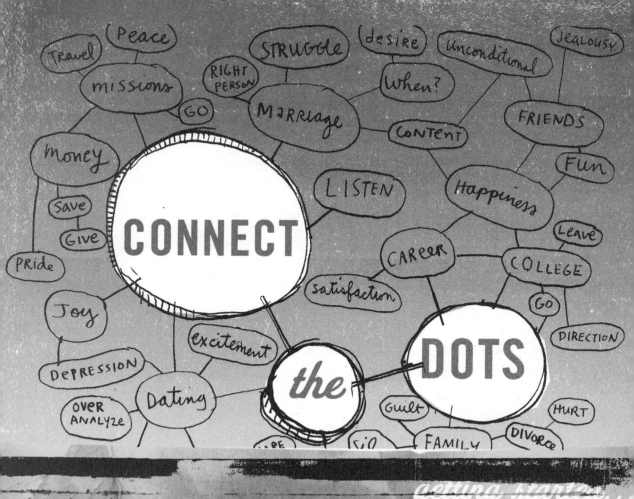

# BEYOND THE BIG THREE

NOTHING SEEMS TO MOTIVATE A SEARCH FOR HIGHER PURPOSE THAN THE "BIG THREE." AS A PASTOR, I HAVE BEEN MEETING WITH YOUNG ADULTS FOR 15 YEARS. DURING THAT TIME, I HAVE LEARNED THAT THE BIG THREE . . .

## WHO SHOULD I MARRY? WHERE SHOULD I WORK? AND WHERE SHOULD I LIVE?—CONSISTENTLY MOVE PEOPLE TO START ASKING THE SEEMINGLY SIMPLE QUESTION: "WHAT IS GOD'S WILL FOR MY LIFE?"

If you are asking these questions, you are certainly not alone—especially if you have spent a couple of years in the workplace and are wondering where you go from here. These are natural questions to ask; it's a part of growing in wisdom. It's a part of defining how you are going to live your life. It's a part of learning what it means to be you on your terms.

But perhaps that is also the flaw in the big three questions. It seems to me that we want to know God's will as long as His will lines up nicely with our idea of what our life should generally be like. That's usually why the big three prompt us to ask the question of God's will—we have in our minds and hearts what we want the answer to be. If that is true, then our question is not really, "What is God's will for my life?" Instead, it's "Does God's will for my life line up with my vision for my life?"

The result is a jumbled blend of our ideas and God's ideas, our desires and His desires, our will and His will. Further complicating the situation is the reality that very few of us have ever seen the proverbial skywriting telling us exactly where to work or who to marry. Many more of us have asked for God to answer our big life questions, but at the end of the day, we have simply had to make a decision with little more than a sense of which direction God wants us to go. The search for any amount of certainty or confidence in God's will has become little more than a pipe dream for most of us. Like a carrot just out of reach of the horse's nose, we ask these big questions hoping to hear a cosmic voice affirm some direction, and yet that voice always seems to be just out of earshot.

Despite this, I firmly believe that God cares deeply about the big decisions of your life. Furthermore, I believe He is incredibly concerned about the mundane, ordinary moments of your life—so much so that perhaps the question God wants us to ask is slightly different than the one we are asking right now.

## MAYBE, BECAUSE GOD WANTS TO BE INTIMATELY INVOLVED IN EVERY DETAIL OF YOUR LIFE, THE QUESTION WE SHOULD BE ASKING IS NOT, "WHAT IS GOD'S WILL *FOR* MY LIFE?" BUT "WHAT IS GOD'S WILL *IN* MY LIFE?"

The difference is huge. If you are asking for God's will for your life, then you are looking for a crystal ball. You want to see into the future to try and find the most prosperous way to go. But if you recognize that God's will is not only *for* your life but *in* your life, then you are choosing to believe in a God who is more than just a fortune-teller. You are choosing to believe that God's greatest call is not for you to be married or single, a preacher or a doctor, to live in Miami or Beijing. His greatest call is for you to follow Jesus—every moment.

Maybe the next several weeks can be a time for you to rediscover that God doesn't just have a plan for you but that God cares deeply about you. Sometimes in the discussion of God's will, we can lose sight of God's love and kindness. If all we are looking for is God's will for our lives, then we betray our perception of God. Our questions reveal that we believe that God is very interested in what we do, where we go, and what we can accomplish on His behalf in the world. But is He only interested in us to the extent that we can be useful to Him?

But I believe God is much more interested in who we are than what we do. For this reason, we do not seek to find answers as much as we seek to find God Himself. It is only through our journey together with Him that we find answers, but amazingly, those answers will become of secondary importance to the great joy and satisfaction of just walking in relationship with God.

That's why it's so vital that we are convinced of God's love for us. Much in the same way that we do not just want answers from Him, He does not just want performance from us. We are meant for each other—us and God—and not just so that we can accomplish each other's desires. We are meant to walk with each other. We are meant to be in each other's lives. We are meant to live deeply together.

I hope that, for you, the end result of *Connect the Dots* is a greater love for, hope in, and commitment to the will of God in your life.

Visit threadsmedia.com to order ~~this~~ this and other Bible studies from Threads.

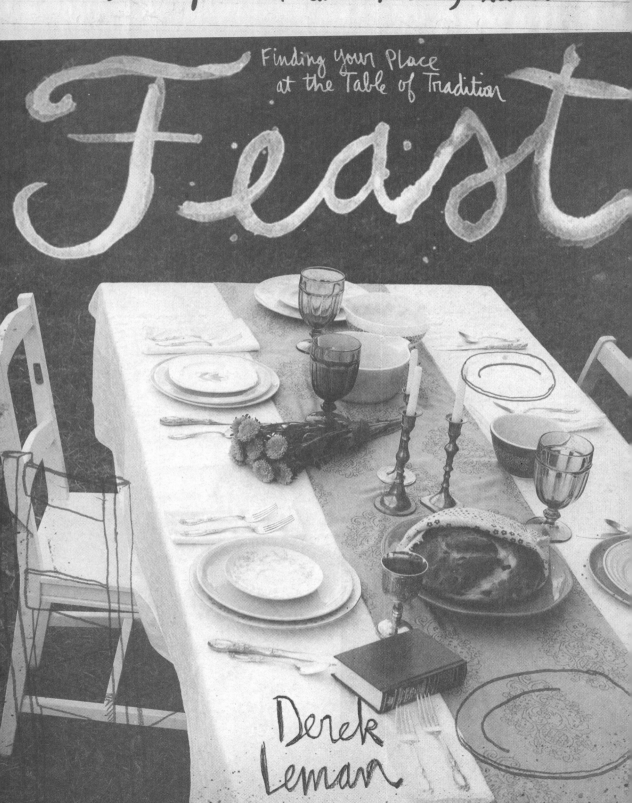

Finding your Place
at the Table of Tradition

# Feast

Derek Leman

# Feast

# Feast

# Remember...

The Book of Judges contains a really disturbing verse: "That whole generation was also gathered to their ancestors. After them another generation rose up who did not know the LORD or the works He had done for Israel" (Judges 2:10). Think about it: In the span of one generation, the chosen people of God forgot their story. They forgot God's story.

How could something like that happen?

You could say it happened because tradition and history were transmitted orally, and because there weren't many hard copies of the permanent records of the nation's history, it slipped away from them. Or you could say that the parents got too busy with the everyday details of life to tell stories to their kids. Or you could say that they got too lazy to prepare the weekly meals and attend the festivals essential to their identity as a people. Whatever the reason, the people forgot where they came from.

**THINK ABOUT IT: IN THE SPAN OF ONE GENERATION, THE CHOSEN PEOPLE OF GOD FORGOT THEIR STORY. THEY FORGOT GOD'S STORY.**

But what's the big deal? I mean, progress is good, and often people get so caught up in tradition that they begin to live in the past. Nobody likes a person—much less an entire culture—that is steeped in "the good ole' days." So what if they stopped telling the stories of their heritage? And so what if they quit eating together weekly on the Sabbath as their grandparents had done? And so what if they stopped prioritizing their yearly festivals and feasts? So what's the big deal?

First and foremost, neglecting these stories and events was a big deal because it was disobedient to the Lord. God commanded His people to pass their heritage down from generation to generation. In fact, that's a big reason why feasts existed in the first place. If you were a kid and you saw your dad waving some branches and a lemon-like fruit in their air, you would naturally be a little curious. The Lord instituted these customs and traditions to provide a regular opportunity for His people to tell the stories of the past.

He did it because remembering is important.

Remembering what happened in the past helps you get through the present and look forward to the future. For the Jewish people, the memory of God's faithfulness in the past served as a yearly reminder of who God was. But it also reminded them of something else. As Tevye said in *Fiddler on the Roof,* "Because of our traditions, everyone of us knows who he is."

**COULD IT BE THAT ONE OF THE REASONS WHY SO FEW PEOPLE, EVEN IN RELIGIOUS CIRCLES, HAVE A FIRM GRASP ON WHO THEY ARE IS BECAUSE THEY DON'T KNOW WHERE THEY CAME FROM?**

Our culture is a lot like the culture described in Judges that forgot the story. Most of us have very few traditions or customs within our family. Maybe we don't prioritize the past because we are obsessed with the latest and greatest piece of technology or dieting or self-help. I can't keep up anymore with what kind of iPod I'm supposed to have, which YouTube video I "need" to watch, and whether I'm still supposed to be on the Atkins or South Beach Diet.

Christian circles are little better. In the name of freedom and relevance, we have tossed out the reminders of who we are. Few Christ-followers celebrate things like Advent or Lent, much less have an appreciation for the Jewish holidays of Passover or Shavout.

Could it be that one of the reasons why so few people, even in religious circles, have a firm grasp on who they are is because they don't know where they came from? Could it be that once again we have stopped telling the stories so essential to understanding not only our heritage but our place in the world and kingdom of God?

That's what *Feast* is about—it's about pulling up a chair at the table of tradition that God has set for His people. It's about remembering that God has been telling the same story throughout history, and so the parts of the story are linked together. It's about reminding ourselves that Jesus was born into a specific culture, that He is a Jew, and that to understand that culture a little more is to understand Him a little more, and eventually, to understand who we are a little more.

Throughout the next several weeks, you are going to learn about the yearly traditions that have been kept for centuries. You will read some things that may seem strange at first, but as you grow in your understanding and appreciation of these Jewish elements, I think you'll start to see not only their significance to the past but how God was preparing the way for Messiah through them.

Through your study, I hope you begin to see that Christianity without Judaism is like a tree without roots.

**SO PULL UP A CHAIR. IT'S TIME TO EAT. AND IT'S TIME TO REMEMBER.**

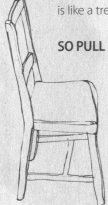

# WHAT IS THREADS?

**WE ARE A COMMUNITY OF YOUNG ADULTS—** people who are piecing the Christian life together, one experience at a time. Threads is driven by four key markers that are essential to young adults everywhere, and though it's always dangerous to categorize people, we think these are helpful in reminding us why we do what we do.

First of all, we are committed to being *responsible*. That is, doing the right thing. Though we're trying to grow in our understanding of what that is, we're glad we already know what to do when it comes to recycling, loving our neighbor, tithing, or giving of our time.

*Community* is also important to us. We believe we all need people. People we call when the tire's flat and people we call when we get the promotion. And it's those people—the day-in-day-out people—that we want to walk through life with.

Then there's *connection*. A connection with our church, a connection with somebody who's willing to walk along side us and give us a little advice here and there. We'd like a connection that gives us the opportunity to pour our lives out for somebody else—and that whole walk along side us thing, we're willing to do that for someone else, too.

And finally there's *depth*. Kiddie pools are for kids. We're looking to dive in, head first, to all the hard-to-talk-about topics, the tough questions, and heavy Scriptures. We're thinking this is a good thing, because we're in process. We're becoming. And who we're becoming isn't shallow.

We're glad you're here. Be sure and check us out online at:

**THREADSMEDIA.COM**

STOP BY TO JOIN OUR ONLINE COMMUNITY — AND COME BY TO VISIT OFTEN!

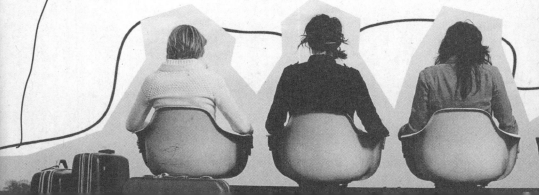